A brilliant book on a bri
Thank you Charlie!

For the world to know y
need two things:

1. to be good at what you do (!) and
2. to be good at promoting it.

One without the other doesn't work.

For example, if you're good at the first but not the second, you become the secret answer to people's challenges – but they don't know about you, so you both lose out.

And of course we all know plenty of self-promoters who don't seem to have any talent or substance behind their blather (yes, I hate them too!).

There are tens of thousands of books on the first of these. But very few on the second...

... And certainly none that come at it from Charlie's angle – how the unnatural, hesitant and therefore often poor self-promoter can become a natural, enthusiastic, brilliant one.

Packed with insights, empathy, charm and new ideas, this book will transform how you promote yourself. I'd go so far as to say it will be a life-changing read for many people.

After all, for you to become more successful, you need more people to think you're more brilliant! This book will ensure they do!

– **Andy Bounds**, award-winning sales expert and best-selling author

The Unnatural Promoter is an exceptional book. It does a fantastic job of reminding both franchisors and franchisees alike what needs to be done to grow a successful business. I highly recommend it.

– **Pip Wilkins**, chief executive,
British Franchise Association

The Unnatural Promoter could have been called *Everything You Need to Know to Succeed in Business*! Charlie Lawson's authentic, engaging and informative writing style is the mark of a true master who knows his subject inside out. I particularly loved the stories and the way Charlie guides us through his practical steps for success. If you want to grow your business in the most cost-effective way possible, this book is a must read.

– **Greg Nathan**, psychologist and author of
Profitable Partnerships

Great book for those who struggle to get their story across. Lots of ideas and useful pointers to make it easy to self-promote, plus some great real life examples.

– **Peter Higgs**, UK national director,
Corporate Connections

Charlie has such an engaging writing style that it feels as though he's having a conversation with you and you alone. His take on self-promotion, something that all business owners need to do, is different to most. He's someone that doesn't find self-promotion easy – but as he's so clearly gone through the learning curve himself, it makes his words all the more relevant and useable.

This book brilliantly articulates how to promote yourself when you don't feel comfortable doing so. Highly recommended.

> – **Mac Srinivasan**, global markets president, BNI

As a young girl I was taught that it was not ladylike to brag about myself and I even discuss it in my book *Business Networking and Sex*. As a business professional I know how important this is. Many of the strategies that Charlie has laid out in this book make it easy to begin practising and learning how to be successful at promotion. Whether you are promoting yourself or getting others to promote you this is the best book I have read on this topic. Ladies, I highly recommend you pick up a copy and find a few good tips that you can implement in your own business.

> – **Hazel Walker**, co-author, *Business Networking and Sex: Not What You Think*

Whether you are the owner of a big or small business, an employee or employer, a natural or unnatural promoter, this book will show you the best places and ways to promote yourself successfully.

The content is engaging and, most importantly, effective. Get it, read it, apply it and I promise you your results will improve!

– **Niri Patel**, national director, fit20 UK

I have interviewed hundreds of businesspeople about introversion and the challenges introverts face in business. A common theme is that many introverts don't like to talk about themselves in public.

If you are an introvert in business who feels icky and uncomfortable being told to promote themselves and your business, read *The Unnatural Promoter*. It will leave you with the comfort, confidence and knowledge to make a difference and promote your business.

It's not just packed with ideas; the case studies show you how they'll work for people like you, and they are detailed enough to put them into practice.

– **Jon Baker**, *The Introvert in Business*

The Unnatural Promoter

CHARLIE LAWSON

The Unnatural Promoter

ISBN 978-1-912300-46-4

eISBN 978-1-912300-47-1

Published in 2021 by SRA Books

A CIP record of this book is available from the British Library.

Printed in the UK

Contents

This one is for you, Dad

Thank you

Robin Schuckmann

There's no way this book would have been
written without you.

Again.

Hannah Milsom and Maggie Mae Lawson
(but definitely not Alfie Lawson –
he doesn't deserve to be mentioned)

Thank you for being amazing x

Foreword

You may well know that Charlie is an Unnatural Networker – he wrote a book about it, after all. But what you may not know is that he also describes himself as an Unnatural Promoter.

When he first told me about this second book, I wasn't initially clear what he meant by being an Unnatural Promoter – but I get it now. Charlie's right – there are so many people out there who don't feel confident to shout about themselves, even though they are extremely talented professionals in whatever it is they do.

They just need the confidence to go out and shout about themselves without feeling awkward. That's where this book comes in. It resonates with me on so many different levels because Charlie understands the insecurities business people feel but are all too often afraid to admit to, let alone address.

The book is packed with stories and honest personal reflections about what it is like to promote yourself and your business when you feel awkward doing so. It is obvious that Charlie relates closely to the emotional roller coaster many of us have been on when trying to grow a business – and that feeling that is so common to entrepreneurs: wanting and needing that phone to ring with potential clients.

In many ways, this book is a forerunner to *The Unnatural Networker*: while that was a great how-to guide for networking, this one focuses on what business owners need to know about just how powerful networking and referral marketing is.

Even if you are not an Unnatural Promoter and you find it easy to shout about yourself, this is a great book that you will learn a lot from. And the chances are, you know some Unnatural Promoters in your network – so why not gift them a copy to help them on their journey?

Lastly, a word on Charlie himself. I've seen him develop as a business owner and leader over nearly 20 years as he's developed within BNI. As National Director for BNI in the UK and Ireland, Charlie walks the talk and has a knack of being able to describe key networking topics in a way that anyone will understand.

I'm delighted and proud to see Charlie doing what he loves and what I taught him to do: helping entrepreneurs to develop and grow through referrals.

Dr Ivan Misner

Founder and chief visionary officer, BNI

Introduction

Recently, I was in a sales meeting in the heart of the City of London. A networking contact had referred me to the prospect, and we were meeting for the first time. Arriving early, I did a couple of laps around the block to kill time and some of my nervous energy, and then went in and introduced myself to the guy on reception.

It turned out that my appointment was in a cab, running late from his last meeting, so while sipping a coffee in the reception area, I was given time to dwell on my thoughts. Would the meeting go well? Would I be able to strike up a rapport? Would he be interested in booking me as a speaker for his upcoming event we'd briefly discussed on LinkedIn?

But once he arrived, we sat down, and we started to talk – everything changed. We got on great, and we talked for some time about the challenges he was facing and how I could help him. He was inspired by my passion and enthusiasm for my subject, and we agreed to do business.

Of course, much of my nervousness before was just down to the anticipation of the meeting – but genuinely, once it started it was fine. It was *easy*.

This got me thinking. The meeting reminded me of all sorts of other occasions where, in a sales context, I have absolutely no problem whatsoever talking about myself and selling my services.

My issue is I don't have enough of those conversations.

I'm not very good at promoting myself

There we are – I said it. In fact, I'm absolutely rubbish at promoting myself.

I believe that I don't get enough sales conversations like my experience in the City of London because of this. I don't like talking about myself. The thought of telling other people how good I am, broadcasting my abilities or publicising myself makes me feel awkward.

I remember very clearly the day that my first book, *The Unnatural Networker* (2014), was published. It was the day of the launch party, and I was nervous as anything.

The event was being held in a big meeting room in the BNI – Business Network International – national office. It was an after-work do, and the team in the office had done a wonderful job getting everything ready. The invites had gone out, the champagne was on ice and the nibbles were all beautifully presented. All I really had to do was turn up, mingle a bit, and say a few words at the right time.

My nerves were partly down to the fact that I would have to do some networking (yes, I really am a very Unnatural Networker). But there was something else. I just didn't feel comfortable with the whole thing.

Firstly, I was going to be the centre of attention. Everyone was there because of *me*. That just doesn't sit well at all. Secondly, and more importantly, not only were people going to be focusing on me, I'd have to talk about myself and my achievements. Of course, people did want to be there. They did want to celebrate the launch. They did want to hear about my experiences writing the book.

It wasn't just the book launch that I found uncomfortable. Ever since, whenever I've been speaking at an event and the organiser has asked me to bring along some books to sell, I get the same pangs of discomfort. I'd much rather the organiser bought a bulk load of books, gave each of the attendees a copy and built the cost into the event ticket price. This means that I don't have to do any sort of promotion (while at the same time selling more books). Of course, recipients of the book then ask me to sign it, and I come over all awkward again...

So why do I feel so uncomfortable? Why am I such an Unnatural Promoter? These questions have driven me to understand myself better since I first asked them. They have led me to want to put down what I've learned in this book. I hope that others out there who feel the same as I do about promoting themselves can find the confidence within themselves to do so.

How this book will help you

This book will focus on various aspects of promoting both yourself and your business. Is there a difference? That depends on the size of your business. For many small business owners, promoting yourself and your business is one and the same thing, because you, the individual, define your business. For larger businesses, it will be less about you, and more about the business as a whole.

Having understood the basic principle of the need to promote yourself and your business, we'll take a look at how effective promotion becomes more about doing business using your relationships, and getting referrals to people who want to use your product or service. As we'll see, doing business by referral is the perfect way for an Unnatural Promoter to promote their business – because other people do it for you!

Getting business by referral requires a number of different building blocks to be put in place: understanding and communicating why you do what you do; communicating effectively about how you help your customers; targeting new customers; and networking with both individuals and groups. We'll cover all of this.

Small business owners may be the primary target for this book, but promotion is still important for bigger businesses, so the tools and techniques included here work for businesses of all sizes. We'll finish up by looking at the self-promotion required as an employee – and as we'll see, much of the content required of business owners applies here too.

Along the way, we'll take a look at some case studies of other Unnatural Promoters – people who have struggled with this concept of self-promotion, but found ways to get around it and become successful.

Promoting Yourself

What is promoting?

If we want to grow a business, we have to be able to promote ourselves. But what does this mean? The word 'promote' derives from the Latin word *promovere* – to move forward. This word was created by combining *pro* (forward) with *movere* (to move). The dictionary definition for 'promote' lists two main meanings:

1. Support or actively encourage (a cause, venture, etc.); further the progress of.
2. Raise (someone) to a higher position or rank.

But, as we saw in the introduction, what we're really focusing on here is self-promotion. Interestingly, a quick Google search of that term leads to a rather more negative description:

self-promotion

noun The action of promoting or publicising oneself or one's activities, especially in a forceful way.

Then it gets worse. You know how dictionaries and reference guides provide an example sentence to show the word in context? This is the one picked here:

She's guilty of criminally bad taste and shameless self-promotion.

Why the negativity? I guess it's focusing very much on the 'self' part – and there's no doubt that there can be a certain 'ickiness' to talking about oneself.

I'm sure that this negative view of self-promoting has contributed to my issues. As a child, if I was playing up or not doing what I was supposed to be doing, I can clearly remember my mum and dad telling me not to 'show off'.

But this worry about promoting myself, or showing off, rears its head all the time. I can think of countless occasions where I've felt uncomfortable talking about myself or posting something about me on social media because I've been worried about what other people may think. Will they think I'm boasting? Will they think I'm being arrogant? Will they be judging me?

Is this because I'm British? There's no doubt that Brits are generally quite reserved. But there are plenty of people I know from the UK who are quite happy to shout about themselves, and plenty of people from other countries who feel just as anxious as self-promotion as I am. The problem is clear though: society views self-promotion as somewhat negative, and we aren't encouraged to do so.

As stigmatised as self-promotion is, if we want to grow a business, we must find a way to do it. Quite frankly, if we haven't got any customers, we haven't got a business – and the only way for people to find out about our business is if we promote it. We'll look at different ways to promote our business shortly, but first let's look at where some of my challenges come from.

A question of confidence

In life, the challenges we face are generally a direct result of learned behaviours from prior experience. Often these experiences will come from childhood or early adolescence. I don't have a lot of recollections from early childhood, so my strongest memories date from my teenage years.

Picture the scene. It's early evening on a Sunday. It's late autumn, so it's cold, wet and dark. It might be miserable outside, but that makes it so much cosier inside. The kitchen is the hive of activity in many family homes, and it's no different on this occasion. My family and I are sitting round the table eating – and because it's the weekend, there's no rush, it's a relaxed occasion.

Round the table are my close family. My mum and dad, my two sisters (one older than me, one younger – middle children *definitely* have it the hardest...), and myself. The conversation flows this way and that. There's enjoyment and laughter, and of course, as is usually the case where people know each other well, a lot of mickey-taking.

So far so good. I'm sure many readers will identify with a standard family dinner table scene.

But it would then typically change – or at least it would in my mind. The conversation would get more serious. It was usually started by my elder sister, Anthea – she's always banging on about something, and my dad would be the first to engage. It might be a current news story, or topical issue, and the conversation would escalate quickly. My mum and Liv, my younger sister, would get involved too. But I didn't.

It wasn't because I didn't want to. It wasn't because I didn't know what they were talking about. It wasn't because I couldn't get a word in edgeways.

No, more often than not, while I knew in my mind what I thought about a given topic – I just didn't have the confidence to say it. The words would come out wrong. My argument would be picked apart. Even when asked a direct question, I'd find it difficult to speak up. Perhaps it was because everyone's eyes were on me.

I'd so often know what I wanted to say – but I just couldn't articulate it. Likely as not, around the family dinner table, I'd resort to my more usual role – that of chief piss-taker, using humour to mask my discomfort of the whole situation.

More recently, I've seen this sort of scenario play out in various settings. With a group of friends on a night out, with Hannah (my other half), when talking ideas through with Tim Cook (my business partner and co-national director at BNI), or indeed in any difficult conversation.

In fact, forget difficult conversations – even sending a message to a light-hearted WhatsApp group can be challenging for me. I've typed what I want to say, but then my finger hovers over the send button, while I get nervous and worry about what people will think.

Wherever I must put myself forward, or my opinion across, I feel very uncomfortable and nervous – and I'd rather run away. I'm an Unnatural Promoter.

Hold on a second...

You may be wondering what's going on. Plenty of people tell me that they cannot believe there's any lack of confidence to promote myself. You may have seen me speak – and when I did so, I wouldn't have looked unconfident. I would have been promoting myself and my message very comfortably. In fact, when I'm speaking in public, I'm in my happy place.

So how can a professional speaker admit to a lack of confidence in what they're saying? Well, several things are going on when I'm speaking:

> ➤ **I'm well prepared.** In most cases, I will have delivered my talk many times before. If it's the first time, I'll have rehearsed it over and over again.

> ➤ I'll likely be speaking about being an Unnatural Networker and generating business. When I'm talking about my own topic, it's so innately part of me and my character, it's not hard for my passion to come through.

> ➤ I'll still get nervous before speaking – nerves are important. If I wasn't nervous, I'd be worried, because the adrenalin improves my speaking performance.

> ➤ **I'm in delivery mode.** Think about you in your business – when you're working for a client, it comes naturally. When I'm speaking on a stage, it comes easily.

Essentially, as I'm in delivery mode, I come across fine. Just as, I'm sure, you do in your business. But if you want your business to grow, there's more to it than just delivery.

We all need to promote ourselves

In business, the only way we can grow is to gain new clients. But if we think we simply deserve to get new clients – in that we're good at what we do, so they should just come to us – nothing will ever happen. I know, it seems unfair...

So, what do we need to do to get a new client? Broadly speaking, it goes something like this:

> ➤ First, we need the phone to ring.
>
> ➤ When it does, we can have a sales conversation. Once in that conversation, as we saw in my example at the start, it is easy. We're in our element as we passionately talk about how we can help a given prospect in their situation. It may or may not lead to business – but that's not the topic of this book.

However, can you spot the potential problem? That's right: what if the phone doesn't ring? There's no chance of having a sales conversation if there's no one to speak to.

We need to be given the opportunity to showcase our business and ourselves. That's what I mean by promoting: getting your foot in the door.

Of course, if I want to get my foot in the door, there are other ways to grow a business too that fall under the general category of marketing. I'm making the assumption now that the basics are all in place – like a brand, a website, a logo and so on. Let's look at some marketing options to see how they work as ways to gain new clients:

Advertising: You can advertise to bring in business – whether through digital online adverts, or via traditional media. There's no doubt that targeted advertising can be very effective – but it also comes at significant cost.

There are two other factors to consider with advertising. Firstly, there's the 'annoyance' factor. How often, when scrolling through your Facebook feed, do you see promotional posts from companies that you just know have been targeted at you? Or, when browsing online, you see 're-marketing' adverts, that are shown simply because you've browsed those companies' websites in the past?

Secondly, there is the long-term relevance of your advertisement. This is key with printed adverts – but how often does your ad appear right next to your competitor's ad? Today's news is also tomorrow's bin liner – so to keep your business in your customer's mind, you've got to advertise again.

PR: Having a newspaper or magazine article written about your business (along with the digital versions), or getting on TV/radio can be an effective way to build your brand. The question is whether this directly leads to sales, or whether it just heightens awareness of your company in the marketplace.

Getting good press coverage is more long term than advertising – the article could still be relevant and therefore useful to you years after it was originally written. That said, building relationships with suitable journalists takes a long time, or you can use a PR agency – but again there is a cost.

Cold calling: You can try cold calling your prospects. This can work to a point: it is a numbers game. If you call enough people, telling yourself that every 'no' brings you one step closer to the next 'yes' – it is possible to get sales opportunities.

But do you enjoy cold calling? Let's face it, there aren't many people who do. Facing the constant rejection is tough. I personally also have another challenge with cold calling. We've already seen that I lack confidence in myself, so the very thought of promoting by effectively forcing myself on a prospect just isn't going to happen.

Email marketing: Emails can be a great way to grow your business, and much like cold calling, if you treat it as a numbers game, you will get some results.

But the need to keep a clean, updated email list, along with having to negotiate the requirements of GDPR legislation, mean that there's a lot more to email marketing than just drafting an email, selecting your contacts and pressing 'send'.

Recruiting a sales person: Much better than having to cold call myself is getting someone else to do it for me! Naturally, hiring a sales person onto your team will (provided they're good) bring in sales – although obviously at the cost to you of their salary.

Of course, many businesses already employ sales staff and entire sales teams. My question to these businesses is whether the sales teams could be even more effective at bringing in business than they are now. Are they, individually, just cold calling, and getting as many rejections as prospects?

Let me be clear – all of these are routes to market. All will bring results. My question though is how much will it cost, and how much time will they take? In any marketing activity, there will be a given return on the investment made, and you've got to weigh that up to see what works best for you.

There's also the fact that I'm an Unnatural Promoter. Advertising, PR or recruiting sales staff are great because I don't need to do it myself. But cold calling to prospect for new business – forget it!

There must be a better way. How much easier would it be if, instead of having to pick up the phone and call people... the phone just rang? Wouldn't it be more cost effective to not have to advertise, run PR campaigns, organise email mailshots or have the expense and hassle of recruiting sales teams? I believe that there are other ways you can use to promote yourself that are less expensive *and* more effective.

What if the phone rang, and on the other end of the line was someone who was in the market for your product or service? Not only that, but they'd also been told about how good you are, and how you could help them? Wouldn't that make life easier?

It may be that you've already got sales teams working for you, or you are in sales within an organisation. The same thing applies – wouldn't it be brilliant if the phone rang and you didn't have to do anything like as much prospecting?

This book is about making the phone ring. It is about what you can do yourself to bring in more and better business that's easier to convert and lasts longer. Even if you are an Unnatural Promoter.

Chapter 1: Action Steps

➤ Make a list of everything you do currently to grow your business – advertising, PR, email marketing, having a sales person on the payroll, networking, etc. You can use this as a starting point to see what you're already doing and what you can build on.

➤ Look at the amount of money and time you spend on each of these and consider the return you get for the time invested and money spent. Are there any interesting learnings that might help you get a better return?

2 Promoting Your Business

What is promoting your business?

So, let's focus on what we mean by promoting ourselves in the context of growing a business. Depending on the size of our business, that could mean we're just promoting ourselves, or it could mean we need to promote ourselves in the context of what we can deliver as a business.

As we've seen already, to grow a business, we need to get sales opportunities. In an ideal world, we need the phone to ring with these opportunities. But it won't happen if we don't talk about ourselves and our businesses! Promotion is all about:

1. **Publicising yourself and your business**
   If people aren't aware you exist, there's no chance of getting sales opportunities. The more visible your business is, the better: more people seeing or hearing about your product or service means more business.

2. **Showing off the value you can add**
   Not only do we need to know what your business is, we need to know about how you help people. What do your clients think about you? Can you prove that you are good at what you do, and do people think you are trustworthy and worth doing business with?

3. **Demonstrating you are an ethical businessperson**
   It is one thing being visible and credible. If people are going to do business with you, they need to know your values and ethics match up to theirs.

4. **Getting people talking about your business**
   As we'll soon see, this is fundamental to the Unnatural Promoter. It is much easier if other people talk about us instead of having to do it ourselves.

5. **Answering the question: 'What do you do?'**
   How often do we get asked this question? All the time – whether it's at a networking event, or in a social setting. Having a good answer that makes it clear who you are and how you add value – the so-called 'elevator pitch' – is crucial.

6. **Delivering your message confidently**
   Self-promotion isn't just about saying something about your business – the message needs to come across *well*. It needs to be confidently delivered in a way that backs up the content of what you're saying.

What we're really trying to do when promoting is give ourselves the opportunity to pitch our business. As we saw with my experience in London, once we're in the sales meeting, we can get across our passion for what we do and how we add value. We just need the chance to show how good we are.

The best way to promote yourself

Picture a good friend. If they were to ask you for some help, would you help them? Of course you would – they are your mate.

But what if a friend needs some help, and although you can't help, you know someone else who could? It is human nature to a) try to help the person who needs something, but also, b) to big up the other person so your friend needing help uses them.

It is easy to talk about someone else. You might not find it easy to shout about yourself – but it gives you pleasure to think that you helped someone else. So you do it.

This is the key thing about being an Unnatural Promoter. You're not comfortable about talking about yourself and promoting what you do. You're not alone – many others feel the same. But there is a way. If other people are prepared to shout about you, *you don't have to do it yourself*. Much better.

Not only that, but there are significant further benefits when other people talk about you.

People tend to believe an independent person, far more than they will than if you talk about your own business. When you're talking about yourself, it can feel like you are bragging. Coming from someone else, it's more likely to be true.

When you book a holiday, what do you tend to do? You might know where in the world to go, but then you get on Tripadvisor. You check out hotels, restaurants, places to visit – and crucially look at reviews. When it comes to a straight choice between two hotels, one with lots of positive reviews, and the other with few or none – it's an easy decision.

What about advertisements? Do you believe them? They are created with one thing in mind – to sell more of the product or service. As such, they are carefully worded and produced to get the results intended. I often think about my kids – when they're watching adverts for the latest toy or games console, how often do they tell me afterwards that they *need* to get whatever it was?

Getting other people to talk about your business is far more powerful than any advert you'll create – because that's the point. *You* created the advert.

Over my time in networking, both in BNI and at all sorts of other events, I've heard business owners stand up and talk about their business. Nine times out of ten, the formula is the same:

- ➤ Hello, my name is...
- ➤ My company is...
- ➤ We can deliver these services...
- ➤ I'd like to be introduced to...
- ➤ Thank you very much.

Business owners are missing such a trick. That third bullet point is where people listening switch off. There are a couple of reasons – one being that hearing a list of someone's products and services isn't very interesting. Secondly, and more importantly in the context we are talking about here, it's just me-focused.

How much better would it be to hear a brief client testimonial or story here? Not only would it be more interesting, we'd hear about how the business owner helped someone. Because we heard it from the other person's point of view, it makes it more likely that that we'll do something about it.

How to get people to promote what you do

But how do you get people to promote what you do? The key here is to go back to my earlier question above: if a friend was to ask you for some help on something – would you help them?

What's the important word here? It's the word 'friend'. You'd be prepared to help them because they are a friend. You have a relationship with them. You care about them. You might not do it for a random stranger, or for an acquaintance.

Now, you may be thinking: 'I just want to grow my business – I don't need new friends!' That's fair enough – but it's the relationship that you have with someone that makes promoting them possible. So, if you want people to promote you – you need to have a good relationship with them. How do you do that?

Without any doubt, the best way is to go networking. Networking is very simple – it is about building relationships with people. Through the conversations you have at a networking event, at a dinner party, over a coffee, etc., you get to know people better.

Once you get to know people, you tend to like them. When you like someone, you build trust. Once you have trust in a relationship, you have a chance of getting people to promote you. The interesting thing then is you often become friends with those people, despite that not being the reason for starting the process in the first place.

The key is to network whenever you can – but does that mean having to attend networking events all the time?

Once an Unnatural Networker, always an Unnatural Networker

I am a shy, introverted person.

You'll be aware of that if you've either read my first book, *The Unnatural Networker*, or seen me at any networking event. Yes, that's right, I'll be the one with my head buried in my phone 'checking my emails' because I don't want anyone to think that I'm uncomfortable about the fact that I'm not talking to someone.

It's taken time, effort and bravery, but through practice, I've become good at networking, and I see returns for my business through it. But do I enjoy it? No! Networking still makes me uncomfortable – it still feels unnatural. I still have to push myself to do it.

Without question, my lack of confidence in being prepared to go up to strangers and engage them in conversation is linked to my challenges in putting myself forward and promoting myself.

The good news is that because Unnatural Promoters can get around their concerns about self-promotion by getting their contacts to do it for them – the tips and tricks learned as a networker help here!

Where can you promote yourself?

The quick answer is *anywhere*. As an entrepreneur, you live and breathe your business almost constantly. In the same way that you can find yourself working on your business at 11pm (because that's when something needed doing, or because you happened to have an idea at that time of the day), you can promote yourself in any given conversation anywhere.

➤ Chatting with a friend?

➤ Speaking to your next-door neighbour?

➤ Family members over for dinner at the weekend?

➤ Having a cup of coffee with a supplier?

➤ Meeting a client for lunch?

➤ Got into a conversation at the supermarket/on a plane/in a lift/walking the dog?

All of these are examples of conversations where you could be promoting yourself and your business. Some of them would clearly be considered social occasions – but is there a rule against talking about 'work stuff'? You certainly shouldn't be hard selling to relatives over the dinner table – but there's no harm in telling people who are close to you about your business and what you want to achieve. If you have a close relationship with someone, then they are already invested in you, and will want to help you.

There are plenty of formal networking events where you can promote yourself, too. Be they in person or online – casual contact networks, strong contact networks, online networks, industry-specific events – all offer a place to have conversations, meet people and build relationships.

These are covered in much more detail in *The Unnatural Networker*.

Essentially though, I believe the best way to promote yourself and your business is by networking – and you can do this anywhere.

Things to avoid when promoting yourself at networking occasions

Having now understood what we mean about promoting ourselves, it is worth having a quick look at a few things that will negatively damage your credibility when it comes to promoting yourself when networking. Remember, there's a fine balance with most things in life, and self-promotion is no different. So bear in mind the following points as you read through the book so you can get the balance right.

> ➤ Always talking about yourself – remember, promotion through networking is about using your relationships with others. If you are only focused on yourself, it will be very transparent, and quickly stop others from wanting to help you.

> ➤ The same thing will happen if you shamelessly self-promote in all circumstances. Sure, you need to be prepared to talk about yourself a bit, and maybe this is an Unnatural Promoter feeling uncomfortable – but being too pushy will put people off from wanting to help you.

> ➤ Hard selling: no one likes being hard sold to, especially if it's in a networking context where the expectation should be trying to help each other. If a networking contact wants to buy from you, they will – so there's no need to sell to them anyway.

➤ Venting, particularly online. Remember that when you post online, your post or comments are there forever. Even if you take them down, they could be screenshotted as a permanent record. If your network perceives that your post damages your credibility and makes it impossible to recommend you, they'll remember it.

➤ Being unprepared. You might think that it isn't the end of the world if you don't have a business card with you when you meet a prospect but being unprepared will definitely affect your chances of success. Always be ready to deliver your elevator pitch – you never know when you might bump into someone who can help your business!

➤ If you want to damage your credibility quickly, don't do what you say you are going to do. This is called follow-up, and it's your first test of credibility after a networking encounter. Remember, you are trying to build relationships, and if you let people down, they won't be likely to promote you.

➤ It is possible to over-commit. Try to do too much networking, and one of two problems may emerge. Firstly, it will become very difficult to keep up the relationships with everyone: you'll end up letting someone down. Secondly, your business can suffer: if you aren't delivering your product or service well enough because you haven't got the time, that's a problem.

Chapter 2 Action Steps

➤ Look at the list of six steps to promote yourself on Page 25. Do you currently promote your business effectively, covering all these points?

➤ Think about the relationships you've built over time that arose from a business context (as opposed to a social/friendly one). How many people have you got a 'friendship' relationship with, despite never intending to become friends?

➤ In the last week, think about how many networking opportunities you had. This may include networking events, but on how many other occasions (social, hobby/interest related, etc.) did you speak to someone, and build a relationship with them?

➤ Do some research into your networking options. Is there a chamber of commerce meeting locally soon? Is there a networking group near you? Does your industry have a professional association that organises events?

➤ Review your profiles on the various online networks – are they up to date, and do they reflect you and your business well?

3 Doing Business by Relationship

So, let's check we're on the same page. First, we've established that self-promotion is important if you want to grow a business. Second, if we don't feel very comfortable about promoting ourselves, then it's much easier to get other people doing it for us. Third, this won't happen unless we build strong relationships with the people we meet.

We're now going to look at some key aspects of building business through relationships. We'll start by looking at referrals, and why they're so good for business.

What is a referral and why are they so good?

A referral is an opportunity to present your business to someone who is in the market for your services, where they are *expecting* your call. It is not a done deal – you still need to go and sell yourself to the prospect, just as with any other business opportunity.

I remember my very first referral as I was setting up my speaker business. The referral came through a good friend, Celia Delaney, although at that time we'd only just got to know each other. As a budding speaker, with something to say but no one to say it to, I just needed an opportunity. One quick introduction from Celia, and I was speaking at a franchise marketing company's event. It was so *easy*.

I cannot overstate how much more comfortable I was when I called the franchise marketing company. There was no awkward and nervous introduction. There was no thinking to myself 'I hope that they don't think I'm wasting their time'. Not only was I not cold calling, I had been recommended to them, so they were looking forward to talking to me when I called.

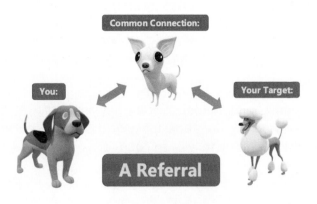

Compare that to what happens when the third party isn't expecting the call – that expectation turns it into a referral. Without that, we might term it a 'lead'. But if the third party has heard about you and is expecting the call, then it is a referral.

Sometimes in business you will receive leads – a contact may tell you that someone they know is looking for your service. When you contact that person, it may turn into business, but it will take a lot more work to turn into a real result. The process of convincing the prospect to use your services is much harder – it's more akin to a cold call. As an Unnatural Promoter, how do you think that makes me feel?!

There's also the way that we, as consumers, approach finding services we need. Obviously, we can search for providers on the internet. But would you want to find a trustworthy solicitor via the internet? What about a dentist, an accountant or an electrician?

People would much rather get referrals for the services they need from trustworthy sources. If someone they know and trust is recommending a business based on their own experience of using them, how much better do we feel about engaging them for ourselves?

Then there are advertisements. We looked at how the public perceive marketing messages in the last chapter, so it's pretty clear that you'd trust what your friends say over an advert. There's no doubt, then, that from the end user's point of view, referrals are better.

Referrals in your business

Think about referrals you've received in your business. You may not have a structured process to receive referrals (or at least not yet), but you will likely have had an existing client recommend you to someone they know, who have now become a client themselves.

> ➤ Was it easy to convert them from a prospect into a client?
> ➤ Have they remained a client in the long term?

In the course of researching this book, I surveyed business owners from all over the world about referrals, and the impact they had on their business. The same themes kept coming out.

Principally, people find it far easier to convert referrals into business than they do other prospects. I compared conversion rates for both referred business and non-referred business (i.e. from advertisements, internet searches, cold calls and so on). The headline figure is that these business owners said referrals are over four times more likely to convert into business.

The other key area I investigated was client retention. Clearly, there are other factors at play here – if customers aren't satisfied in any number of ways, they won't stay. But my hypothesis was that if business originally came from a referral, it is likely that the client would stay longer.

The numbers did reflect this – I compared customer retention rates for referred and non-referred business, and I found that retention is 12 per cent higher when the client originated from a referral. I believe this is because the element of trust, which originates from how the customer met the business provider in the first place, continues throughout the lifetime relationship between the two parties. Once a customer has found a good supplier that was recommended to them, why change?

So, for you as the business provider, referrals are a great way to do business – much easier to convert because you've been recommended to the prospect, and likely to remain a client for longer, again because you've been recommended.

We've already seen how referrals are better for the end user – the trust that comes from being recommended by someone we know makes a huge difference. But there's one other person we should consider here – what about the person in the middle of the referral?

That person, the referrer, is crucial – without them, the referral doesn't happen. The end user doesn't get a trusted recommendation and must rely on an internet search. The business provider doesn't get the opportunity, and so loses out on business.

What's in it for the referrer? Why are referrals good for them?

There are two benefits that I can see. Firstly, there's the fact that the person in the middle gets to help two different people. They have matched up one person's need and another person's ability to cater for that need. Everyone has slightly different motives for wanting to help, but giving referrals and making connections feels good.

Secondly, there's the issue of credibility. If I can help solve someone's problem by introducing them to a business that fixes it for them, how will they look at me? Will I have strengthened our relationship? Of course!

In the same way, if I can introduce a business owner to a new client that's easy to convert and stays a long time, how will they perceive me? Again, I will have strengthened our relationship, and there's every chance that the other person might look to reciprocate (we'll investigate this in more detail shortly).

There's a huge reward for whoever is in the middle of a referral – but at the same time, it is important to remember that there's also a big risk. While it's great when everything works out well, what happens if the referral goes wrong?

If this was business that hadn't come through a referral, then there might be some sort of a complaint, or a withholding of payment, and maybe some negative word of mouth for the service provider to deal with.

But in the case of a referral, all that negative stuff can pale into insignificance in comparison to the reputation of the referrer – me, the person in the middle. My reputation is on the line because I've recommended the person who has now gone on to do a bad job. That damages my credibility, and I've got no control over that – other than not making the referral in the first place.

Let's look at a couple of concepts that help to explain how we can mitigate against this reputational risk, and that will also help show the best way to get the referrals we need to build a business.

Understanding the Referral Confidence Curve

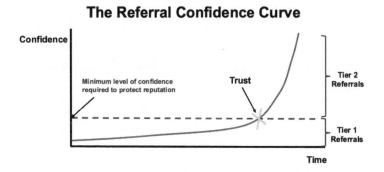

Take a look at the Referral Confidence Curve. On the horizontal axis is time. You'll note that there is no scale – the time shown could be a month, it could be a year. On the vertical axis, there is confidence. Again, there is no scale – mainly because I have no idea what a unit of confidence looks like!

What we mean here is the amount of confidence a potential passer of a referral needs to have in you and your business. As we've just seen, the risk is on them: not because there's an assumption that you will do a bad job, but until they know you better, they've got to protect their reputation.

To pass a referral then, there needs to be a certain level of confidence in you, as shown by the dotted line. As such, you will always start near the bottom of the confidence scale.

Until the trust point is reached, it is always going to be difficult to pass a referral. But once at the point of trust, referral-passing is easy. Not only do I not have to worry about protecting my reputation – passing a referral will actually *enhance* my standing.

Below the trust point, there will be *some* referrals. But they're only ever going to be for something low risk. Perhaps it will be trying out your service personally – once you've experienced the product or service, it will be easier to recommend. This is a tier one referral.

But above the trust point, you can see the curve grows exponentially. Once trust is there, you will potentially receive referrals to other people (i.e. it won't be someone just trying you out). This is a tier two referral. Then, those other people will potentially refer you on to *their* contacts. That is a tier three (or four, or five and so on) referral.

How referrals build over time

Caroline Connolly, a health and safety professional, is now getting plenty of good quality referrals for her business – but it wasn't always that way.

She told me about a referral she received some eight years ago, very early on in her networking career. A painter/decorator contact of hers, Thomas, asked her for a simple first aid course for his business. This was very much a bread and butter piece of business – something she did regularly that brought in a little income, but nothing to get excited about.

But, having done the work, Thomas referred Caroline on to a friend of his. His friend ran a garden landscaping company and wanted a health and safety statement for his business. Again, this was basic work, easy to complete, but not going to take Caroline's business to the next level. Not thinking a huge amount more about it, Caroline did the work.

This landscape gardener was a member of the National Association of Landscape Professionals, and he referred Caroline to become a supplier to the association. She was asked to prepare a templated health and safety statement for the hundreds of members of the association. The original referral, remember, was to a painter/decorator – it was now starting to get a bit more interesting.

The contact Caroline worked with at the association was so pleased with what Caroline produced that she referred her on to a friend of hers, who worked for a large shopping centre. She started doing health and safety audits for them.

But it didn't stop there. Her contact at the shopping centre referred her to a place called Airfield Estate – a big country house with a working farm, visitor attractions, restaurants, wedding venue and so on. Airfield Estate now bring Caroline in once a year for two weeks to train all their 200 or so staff on health and safety.

All of that came from one referral to a painter/decorator. Caroline told me that the original referral has now brought in work well over €300,000 to her business – so far!

Two things struck me about Caroline's story. Firstly – how cool is that?! Secondly, and more importantly, is the number of tiers of referral the story encompasses. By the time the referral had got to Airfield Estate, it was a fifth-tier referral – in other words, she had gone through four completely separate other referrals to get there.

Visibility, Credibility, Profitability

The second concept to guard against reputational risk in referral passing is a process we speak about in BNI: Visibility, Credibility, Profitability. It shows you the stages you'll need to go through to create a worthwhile networking relationship.

It all starts with **Visibility**. Imagine you're meeting someone for the first time. Are you going to give them a referral? Are they going to refer you? Of course not. At this point, you're just taking in information on the other person. What sort of person do they appear to be? Are they friendly and do they greet you with a smile? How are they dressed? What sort of conversation do you have? Are they only interested in talking about themselves, or are they keen to hear from you?

The Visibility stage could continue at your subsequent meetings, as you carry on getting to know one another. Visibility is exactly as it sounds – the two of you are *visible* to each other, but that doesn't mean you feel you know them enough to share your contacts and pass them referrals. And vice versa.

So at some point you will move into the **Credibility** stage. This is where you will both find out whether you can trust the other person enough to refer them. Credibility can be gained in various ways:

> ➤ You might try their services out for yourself. Likely this will be a small job, just to see how they operate.
>
> I heard a wonderful story about a carpenter who was trying to build his business through referrals. He told me that when he got his first referral, he was so disappointed. It was from

a property developer, who asked him to make some doorstops – little wooden wedges, worth pennies, and he could do them in his sleep. He wanted to get referrals to build a whole kitchen or bedroom suite – and all he was being asked to do was a doorstop!

But he did the work – and in so doing demonstrated his professionalism. Shortly afterwards, he was given another referral by the property developer. This one was to install fitted wardrobes in a block of flats. Thirty of them! It had certainly been worth proving how credible he was as a carpenter by doing the doorstops.

➤ You might continue to build a relationship on a one-to-one basis. As you get to know each other more, and understand what sort of person they are, who their friends are, what their interests are, what their ethics are like and so on, you may well find they become credible enough to refer. That said, you might still want to try them out for yourself first.

➤ You might hear them speak about their business. Many networking events allow you to do this, and we'll look into speaking as a way of promoting yourself in more detail in Chapter 10. But you'll be able to pick up a lot of information about whether they are credible from what you hear.

➤ Testimonials from other clients are a great way of building credibility – especially if, as you get to know your contact, you also know who the testimonials are from.

➤ How they follow up: this is a key concept in networking, and essentially it is all about what happens after a networking situation. If you meet someone at an event and agree to send them an email... send them the email! Whatever you say you're going to do, make sure you do it.

Because what happens if you don't? Follow-up is the very first test of credibility, and there are plenty of networking relationships that don't blossom because they fail at the very start.

It is only once you've been through Visibility and Credibility that you can reach the stage of **Profitability**. This is where the networking relationship is strong enough both in the sense that you know each other, and you trust each other to be able to pass referrals back and forwards.

Unfortunately, so many people try and jump the process. Think about it – if you haven't got visibility, how on earth can you try to get to profitability? That's like me contacting Sir Richard Branson, completely cold, and trying to do business.

Let's say you've got visibility, but no credibility (yet). In this case, it is just too early to ask for referrals. This is where many people go wrong, as they haven't got the patience to let credibility build over time.

In their book, *Business Networking & Sex (Not What You Think)*, the authors Ivan Misner, Hazel Walker and Frank DeRaffele (2012) looked at the differences between men and women in networking. They found that men were much more likely to try and jump from visibility to profitability, thus harming their networking efforts as they don't get referrals because they don't deserve them yet.

Equally, women sometimes don't ask for referrals when they've got easily enough credibility to move into the profitability stage. Again, this can harm their networking efforts – but this time, they don't get referrals because they're just not being bold enough to ask for them.

You may be thinking that there are certain similarities here between networking and dating. I've lost count of the number of times I've been told that I could offer great dating advice! Without doubt, there are parallels to be drawn – but perhaps the biggest one here is that if you want to build a long-term relationship (in networking or in life), you've got to take the time to build it carefully and patiently.

There's one last thought on the VCP process. It is tempting to look at it as a formula, V + C = P. In other words, if you gain Visibility, then build Credibility, you will automatically get Profitability. It doesn't work like this!

VCP works as a process. My good friend Phil Berg has a great way of describing how it really works. Imagine VCP represent three different rooms, like this:

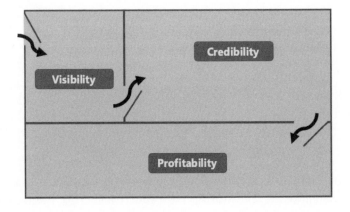

You want to get into the Profitability room, but to do that, you must pass through the Visibility and Credibility rooms first. There are no other doors. There are no other short cuts. It takes time. Not only that, but it is almost as though there is a guard on each of the doors, checking that you have reached the correct level of visibility to move on to credibility, or the correct level of credibility to move on to profitability.

One last thought on VCP: taking Phil's analogy of each step being a different room, what stage are you in if you don't even go into the Visibility room in the first place? That's right: invisibility. No one can see you, and no one is going to promote you at all.

Farming vs hunting

Given the time it takes, it is vital to come at networking and generating referrals with a farming attitude rather than a hunting approach. Picture a lion in Africa. The lion thinks, upon waking up, that they're feeling hungry. As are the rest of the pride. So they'd better go and find some food. They then go and hunt some poor stag or antelope. There's a chase scene, a kill scene, and then there's food for all the family. What happens the next day? The same thing – it is a subsistence way of living.

Okay, a simplistic way of looking at it – but some people approach their networking in a similar way. They find a group of people. They think they can do some business with them. They then hunt round the group, looking to do as much business as they can.

But there will only be a few people that can and want to do business with them. At that point, they've got to go and find another group of people to prey on. Unfortunately, they're missing the whole point of networking. While it is fine to do business with the people you meet, it's much better to try to get to know them well and to be introduced to their contacts.

Farming is a much better approach. When she was about four years old, my daughter, Maggie Mae, and I planted some carrot seeds in the garden one weekend. She was very excited about growing our own carrots, and the thought of being able to get food from out of the ground, in our own garden, fascinated her.

So we planted the seeds. By the end, there appeared to be more mud on Maggie Mae than in the ground... But once we were done, we looked at the patch of ground with satisfaction. Shortly after though, I noticed that Maggie Mae had gone a bit quiet. I asked her what was up.

'It's going to take ages for them to grow,' she said in a sad voice.

She wanted to harvest them then and there! Of course, it doesn't work like that. We talked about making sure the seeds got plenty of water, and then as the plants grew, they got sunlight and insects didn't get at them. Then, over time, the carrots would grow, and after some more time, they'd be ready to pull out of the ground and eat.

Networking requires a similar approach. When you meet people, you need to take time to build the relationship. You've got to look after it, and 'feed and water' it as necessary. You've got to continue to build the relationship continuously. The question is: how long will this take?

How long does it take to get referrals?

A recent study by Jeffrey A. Hall (2018), a University of Kansas professor, looked at the amount of time it takes to become friends with someone. Given the need to build great relationships to become friends, and the need to build great relationships to pass referrals and do business – it is worth considering what Jeffrey Hall's study found.

He argued that there were three stages of friendship, and different amounts of time were required to reach each of those stages.

When we meet someone new, they are an acquaintance. The first stage of friendship is when we reach what Jeffrey Hall describes as 'casual friendship'. This is where you've got to know someone, but there isn't any real depth to the relationship.

Hall's survey found that it takes 50 hours of time spent together to reach a stage of casual friendship. Consider that for a moment – that's not 50 hours since you met someone, that's 50 hours of quality time spent with them. That might include time chatting, eating, having a drink, competing in a sport/activity – whatever. The key is time together.

The next stage is 'good friends'. Hall found that it takes 90 hours of quality time spent together to reach this point. Finally, there's 'close friends'. This takes 200 hours to get to.

So, what about referrals? There is no way that having the equivalent of a casual friendship will get you the referrals you want. I would argue that at the very least, your relationships need to be comparable to somewhere approaching Hall's good friends level.

That means up to 90 hours of quality time together building your relationship. When you consider that you might sit down for an hour over a coffee, or spend pockets of time here or there on the phone, or might see them occasionally at a social event – it will take a long time to build up the requisite 90 hours-plus.

Getting referrals faster

In a sense, I've been trying to put across the challenges you will face in building a business by relationship. We've looked at several concepts that have demonstrated that it takes time to get referrals.

➤ The Referral Confidence Curve showed us that we must get to the point of trust before we're going to get the types of referrals that we really want, and it is impossible to tell exactly when this will happen.

➤ The Visibility, Credibility, Profitability process demonstrated the stages that need to be gone through before getting to a point where we receive referrals.

➤ The concept of farming versus hunting is very clear about how it takes time to get business from networking.

➤ Professor Hall's study indicates that it takes up to 90 hours to build the relationships necessary to get referrals from networking.

Hopefully the message is clear! But if you're still with me, and up for the job of learning how to promote yourself effectively, that's a start.

The Unnatural Promoter

But there is one way to help speed the process up: *giving* referrals to people in your network wherever possible. Networking success, as we've seen, comes from building quality relationships. There is no quicker way to build a relationship with another person in business than by trying to help them grow their business. The more you give, the more you grow the relationship.

This is down to a social psychology norm: the law of reciprocation. In his book, *Influence: The Psychology of Persuasion*, Robert Cialdini (2007) talks about this law. He says that human beings have a universal tendency to feel compelled to repay or reciprocate when given a gift – whether that is a material object, a kind deed, or an act of generosity.

Think about the last time you were invited to a friend's house for dinner. What did you do afterwards? You invited them to come to your house next time. What about the last gift you received, perhaps for Christmas or on your birthday? You thought to yourself: 'Oops, I didn't get them something, I need to return the favour!'

Referrals work in the same way. A referral is an act of kindness, where you try and help someone. Sometimes making that referral will increase your credibility – but not always. But what giving a referral will do is make people think that they'd like to find you a referral in return.

So, if you want to receive more referrals, and speed up the process of getting them – the best thing you can do is give more referrals. In BNI, we call this Givers Gain.

Givers Gain is the founding philosophy of BNI, and the most important of its core values. It means that if I can pass business to you, you will pass business back to me in return. It is based on the principle of what goes around, comes around. Givers Gain doesn't usually work in direct terms: if I pass a referral to you, I'm not going to expect a referral straight back from you the next time I see you. However, I can expect something back from the group.

One word of caution here: it is never a good idea to give with the expectation of receiving. It will become very transparent that you are only trying to help yourself, and you have no real interest in helping your networking contacts.

If you can give, keep giving, and keep giving (and then give some more) – it will come back to you. You don't necessarily know when, and even who from, but it will come. It's a mindset, a way of living your life.

I appreciate that this doesn't help you plan out exactly how your business is going to grow. But as we'll see over the next few chapters, there are various things you can do to make it more likely you're going to receive referrals. Just as long as you keep giving.

Chapter 3: Action Steps

➤ Think about referrals you've received in your business. Were the opportunities easier to convert? Did you retain the customer for longer?

➤ Think about any referrals you've given. How did they work out? Was your credibility enhanced with either the business provider or the end user?

➤ Make a list of some of your networking contacts and define a) where you are on the Referral Confidence Curve with each of them and b) whether you are in Visibility, Credibility or Profitability with them.

➤ Think about your network, and the two people that you know best, both as a pure friend, and as someone you've got to know on a business level over time. How many hours of quality time have you spent with each of them?

➤ Think about referrals you've given. How many have you given in the last couple of months? Who could you identify in your network that you could help by finding them a referral?

4 Knowing Your Why

Let me tell you about Paul Connelly.

He started his driving school business shortly after being made redundant from his job as a lorry driver. Initially he wasn't sure how to grow his business: he got a few clients here and there from his (then) franchisor.

Now, he runs a well-established business, with 11 vehicles on the road, with contracts for companies across the country. Along the way, he has bought out other driving schools, allowing him to develop his business further.

Sounds like a business success story, doesn't it? Well it is – and Paul puts a huge part of his success down to promoting himself successfully through networking. But there's something far more fundamental that has helped Paul to be successful.

Delve deeper into Paul's story, and you find out about his childhood. He had a tough upbringing, with an abusive father. He never felt safe at home and was constantly having to try to avoid him.

What does a driving instructor do? They help make the roads safer. Paul does what he does because living in a safe environment is something that is so important to him, having not had it when he grew up.

Whether we realise it or not, many of us are pulled towards doing what we do for a reason. Somewhere in our upbringing, our understanding of our own world creates an inbuilt belief system that remains very strong throughout our lives.

Paul didn't consciously become a driving instructor because of the relationship he had with his dad. But the way he looks at the world around him and the kind of life he wants to lead most certainly has a bearing on his professional career now.

Trying to create a safe environment is Paul's 'Why'. At a fundamental level, your Why is your subconscious reason for doing whatever it is that you do.

So, what is my Why? Well, we covered that back in Chapter 1. Remember the story about me sitting at my family dinner table, not having the confidence to speak up when the conversation was going around?

I wish I had had more confidence to get my point of view across – but it meant that I felt somewhat marginalised, and that people didn't want to hear what I had to say.

This affected me a lot when it came to my teenage years of socialising, and going to parties, bars and so on. I never felt confident to go and talk to girls, for example, because I thought they wouldn't be interested in talking to me.

This lack of confidence came with me when I went into my professional life – for instance, I often didn't feel confident to put my point of view across in meetings.

And of course, it became a massive issue for me when it came to networking. In that situation, you've *got* to talk to people, but of course I didn't feel confident because I thought I'd have nothing interesting to say.

Over time, I have, of course, realised that I do have *something* interesting to talk about: I'm sure my better half, Hannah, wouldn't have put up with me for all these years if I hadn't (and that does mean that I did pluck up the courage to talk to at least *one* girl...)

I do, of course, still suffer from confidence issues around promoting myself – but my mission in life is to help the vast number of people who are, like me, Unnatural Networkers.

Much like Paul Connelly didn't initially become a driving instructor because he wanted to make the world a safer place, I didn't start working within networking because I realised that I lacked confidence and I wanted to help other people do the same.

No, I started doing what I do because it was the right business model for me at the right time in my life. It was only later that I realised that I'm in a business that is tailor-made for Unnatural Networkers who lack confidence to network with other people, and that I could show them the amazing power of promoting their business through referrals.

Why is knowing your Why so important?

Knowing your Why really is important. When you're clear on your Why, your passion for what you do shines through. This is what gets people wanting to use your services or being prepared to promote your business and find you referrals. Let's look at some key reasons why this is the case:

1. Other people are more likely to want to help you

Take Paul Connelly again for a moment. Imagine at a networking event he tells you that he's looking for referrals to grow his driving school business. Now it's difficult to do this next bit – but disregard what I told you about his upbringing and family situation. All you know is he wants to get referrals to grow his business.

Of course, this is hypothetical and you don't know Paul – but how inclined are you to want to help him and get him referrals?

What if, in fact, you are armed with the knowledge that Paul is trying to make a difference in the world to make it a safer place, and he's doing that because he suffered hardship and didn't have a safe family environment? Does that make a difference?

I think it does. It shows his passion for what he does. It is this depth of understanding about you and why you do what you do that means people really understand who you are.

Not only that, but the more we tell our own story of our Why, the more others are likely to share it because it reaches an emotion that empowers others to share the story again and again.

2. Businesspeople need to be inspired

Picture yourself in a sales meeting. You've prepared your pitch, you look the part, you're ready to go. How would it feel to start talking about your childhood or something from when you were in your adolescent years?

You might think it would feel out of place and weird but try it. The person on the other side of the desk to you might be a prospect that could become your next most important client, so the thought of taking the conversation down a personal route wouldn't feel right.

But they're also human. They will connect with human emotions that drive your behaviour. They may not think the same way – but they will understand where you're coming from.

Not only that, but they are a decision-maker. The best way to get them to decide in your favour is to inspire them. You are far more likely to do this if your passion comes to the fore. Your passion comes from your Why.

3. It's clear what you stand for

A key part of building strong relationships with contacts in your network is to know what they stand for. It helps generate credibility and a desire to help them.

Take, for example, Kate Bourne from Case Study 1. Assuming you haven't read her case study yet, I'll tell you that she started a baking business. She networked to get referrals to grow it. She's very good at what she does. Would you be prepared to refer her? On the strength of that, probably not. Now – go and read her case study.

Done? Would you be prepared to refer her now? I think it's much more likely.

With an understanding of what happened to her and her daughter, you now know what Kate stands for, and why she did what she did. That makes it much easier to refer her.

4. It's more fun (and interesting) to associate yourself with passionate people

Well it is, isn't it? When people are passionate about what they do, they're more engaging and interesting. This on its own can help make networking events much more enjoyable.

Sometimes in life, the reason why we do what we do gets lost, and we get caught up in the day-to-day grind of our profession. But, if we can think back to when we started, we can remind ourselves of the reason why we do what we do. A time when we were excited about going into business and had a clear reason why we did so.

This is why, when training people how to network, I encourage them not to ask 'What do you do?', but instead 'How did you get into what you do?' It's much more interesting that way.

Haven't I heard this Why concept before?

Hopefully you have, but if you haven't, I strongly recommend what is, in my opinion, the best book there is on leadership in business. Simon Sinek's *Start with Why* (2011) is what helped inform a lot of the concepts of this chapter. If you haven't got time to read the book, then you can check out the third most watched TED talk of all time – Simon Sinek's 'How great leaders inspire action'.

Sinek's point is that people don't care *what* you do, or even *how* you do it. They care *why* you do what you do. The problem is, many businesses only really talk about *what* and *how*.

To make your messaging compelling, he argues that the order should be: Why, How, What. Take these examples from when I'm pitching my services to organisations to speak and motivate their teams about networking. I could say:

I will help your teams get better results from networking *[what]*, and I'll do that by helping them to get over their fears of attending a networking event by showing them how an Unnatural Networker does it *[how]*.

Alternatively, how about this approach:

The world is full of businesspeople who don't feel comfortable talking to strangers, whether that is because they are shy and introverted, or because they lack the confidence to do so. But that means they struggle to network effectively. I believe that everyone should be able to benefit from the incredible results networking can create *[why]*. I'll do that by helping them to get over their fears of attending a networking event by showing them how an Unnatural Networker does it *[how]*. The result will be that your teams get better results from networking *[what]*.

Do you see the difference?

What's your Why?

How clear are you on your Why? Are you like Paul Connelly, and you've connected what you do now with happenings in your past? Or are you like most people, without a clear sense of why you get out of bed in the morning?

It is important to be clear about it too: how often do you see people that aren't happy in the job they do? How many people are leading unfulfilled lives because they are not passionate about what they do? The answer is way too many.

So, let's look briefly at the process for finding your Why. Before we do, I strongly recommend you return to Simon Sinek for help. He wrote (along with his co-authors David Mead and Peter Docker) a follow-up to *Start with Why*: it's called *Find your Why* (Sinek et al. 2017), and it's a practical workbook guide to doing so.

Here's the basic approach though:

1. **Think about your life, and recount stories from your life that may have shaped how you feel about the world. It is particularly worth focusing on stories from your formative years, as difficult as it can be sometimes to remember them or know what to focus on.**

Recently I was involved in a 'find your Why' discovery session with a member of my mastermind group. I can't share all the details, but for the purpose of telling you the story, let's call him Steve. Steve's business focuses on change and innovation.

The session started with Steve telling us that he just isn't an emotional type of person. While he understood the concept of Starting with Why, he wasn't at all convinced that this approach would lead to him discovering his own Why.

After answering a number of questions about his life, we found out that Steve had run away from home at about age 13. He was from a single parent family (his parents had split when he was six months old), and when we asked why he had run away, he couldn't recall anything specific that had triggered it. It was really just a build-up of consistent messaging being fired at him in his childhood: he was dissatisfied with the status quo.

Within just a few minutes of questioning, we had discovered a key part of the reason why Steve did what he did. When it came together, everyone just knew we had arrived at the key point – it just felt *right*.

One other lesson that came out was that it is easier to do with multiple people in the room. That way, I started asking questions, and when I dried up, other people would come in and continue the questioning. It was quick-fire, gut instinct-type stuff, rather than laboriously trying to work it out.

2. **Once you have got your Why, you need to think about how you deliver it. This is where you bring in your take on what you do and how it adds value. Take my example of teaching people how to network. My 'how' isn't just that – my focus is to look at networking through the lens of an Unnatural Networker.**

What expertise do you bring to your topic? This may come from your core values, your point of view, your experience, or even your habits. Again, consider your history to help you find the answers. How do you work? What skills do you have? What experience have you gained? What are your values, and how do they affect the work you do?

3. Once you have got your Why – share it! It may help you to write it down, somewhere you can see it easily. But get into the habit of telling as many people as you can – as we've already seen, this will help you inspire your contacts to want to promote you.

Helping a team find its Why

Last year, I ran a retreat with BNI's UK and Ireland franchisees. We'd been working on leadership, and Simon Sinek's *Start with Why*, and while BNI has a very clear set of mission and vision statements, as well as its core values, we felt that one thing was missing.

While some of the 50 or so franchisees present were relatively clear on their own Whys, we felt the team wasn't coordinated and clear on its purpose. Why did we come together as a team? Why does the team want to do what it does?

Over the course of a day, we followed the process outlined in *Find your Why*:

1. We told each other specific stories of when we felt most proud to work within BNI.

2. Then, using the stories we'd told, we looked for specific contributions that BNI had made to the lives of others.

3. We then looked at what these contributions had allowed other people to go on to do or to be. We wanted to find out the impact of what had happened in the story.

4. Drawing themes from the stories, the contributions, and the impacts, we drafted Why statements that used the format:

Doing X so that Y

X was the contribution that BNI makes, while Y was the impact or effect of that contribution.

5. The group then whittled the statements down to two Why statement options, trying to best capture the contribution that BNI makes to society.

6. Finally, we had help from a copywriter to turn the Why statements into one, all-encompassing version.

The end result was:

Developing people and businesses to change lives and enrich communities.

This phrase has since become widely used and helps BNI franchisees articulate why they do what they do. It helps them show their passion every day.

Saving the world

When it comes down to it, most people's Why ends up being how they will save the world. Clearly, most people don't *actually* save the world – but you're looking for why what you do is important. Paul Connelly is trying to make the world a safer place. I'm trying to make the world a better place for unconfident people.

You see – saving the world!

Your version of saving the world is your cause. Some people will buy into that, some people won't. That doesn't matter – it's the people who do buy into what you do that will follow you and promote you. For Unnatural Promoters, knowing your cause and telling people about it helps.

Chapter 4: Action Steps

➤ If you haven't already done so, make Simon Sinek's *Start with Why* the next book that you read. Clearly finish this one first though...

➤ Think through your life to help you work out your Why. You're looking for the key events that helped shape you to think the way that you do. It can be much easier to do this in discussion with people that know you well.

➤ Once you've discovered your Why, share it widely!

Case Study 1
Kate Bourne

Kate Bourne is a very Unnatural Promoter. That much was very clear when we had a quick phone call – and so much so that I asked her if she'd be prepared to meet up and have a proper chat about being one.

As I interviewed her, I genuinely couldn't believe it. She answered all my questions with exactly the same answers that I would have given. It was almost as if I was looking in a mirror in terms of the responses I received – if only mirrors provided audible responses.

The background

Kate launched her bespoke cake-baking business, Violets Kitchen, a few years ago because she wanted to pursue her passion for baking. She'd worked in various jobs, most recently in marketing for a gym – but they weren't fun, and she wanted to do something she was truly passionate about while being in control of her own destiny.

What makes it particularly interesting is that Violets Kitchen started shortly after Kate had her daughter, Amelie. She had wanted to work more at home so she could be there for Amelie, but the business became inextricably linked to Amelie.

Kate suffered a terrible experience when Amelie was born. Without getting into detail, due to complications in childbirth, Kate nearly died, and she had to fight for her life for several weeks afterwards.

She is healthy and well now, and Amelie is a typical, bouncy three-year-old – but the experience she went through means that Kate views the success of her business through the eyes of her daughter. She now wants it to succeed not just because she needs to earn a living: it's a matter of proving to Amelie what's possible if you put your mind to it, follow your passions, and believe that you can thrive.

How Unnatural a Promoter?

The short answer is *very*. The longer answer is that the trauma surrounding Amelie's birth massively affected Kate's self-confidence. She had never been confident in herself – but her experiences made it so much worse.

She knew that she had to get her business promoted – that much was clear. As a new business, she had to get herself known in the marketplace, and when baking high-end, bespoke cakes for weddings and events, good word of mouth for the business was essential.

The problem was Kate just didn't feel comfortable shouting about herself. It wasn't that she didn't know what she was talking about – she knew she was good at baking and her designs spoke for themselves.

But the thought of putting her ideas into the public domain and feeling that people would be judging her stopped her from getting all sorts of opportunities. She didn't even want to set up a Facebook page for the business because of the fear of what people might say.

Perhaps the biggest challenge for Kate was her fear of public speaking – the thought of having to promote herself and at the same time having to do something she was scared of meant that Violets Kitchen didn't grow initially.

So what happened?

It just had to be a case of mind over matter. When she reflected on her reason for starting the business – her daughter – she knew she just had to promote herself. There was no way she could countenance going back to her old job and being (in her eyes) a failure to Amelie.

A routine appointment to solve some aches and pains at her chiropractor changed the course of her business as she was invited to come and network at an event in Stockport, her home town.

Initially, the old doubts surfaced. The lack of self-confidence, the worry about having to express her opinions, the thought of having to speak in public. But she then discovered that other people were prepared to help her and talk about her to their contacts.

As she built relationships with the people she met networking, she found it was like a virtuous circle. Striking up the confidence to share the message with her networking contacts meant that she saw and heard them positively talk about her business. This increased her confidence that she was good at what she did, and that spurred her to promote herself more when networking.

The best example of that working was when one of her contacts, Pete Longbottom, referred her to a wedding planner. She would have loved to have had an 'in' with her – but it was impossible to get near her. The wedding planner appeared to be a closed shop – she had her people she worked with and it was very hard to break in.

But with Pete being prepared to promote her, she got a chance to have a meeting with the wedding planner – and now Kate is one of those preferred suppliers being recommended on a regular basis to couples soon to be married.

Kate still hates the public speaking – but her advice here for anyone in her situation is you've just got to go for it. It will likely be terrible the first time! It will get easier. Plus, remember that no one else knows what you're going to say. So it doesn't matter if you miss something out!

Kate is still an Unnatural Promoter. She always will be. In fact, when I drafted this and ran it past her to check she was happy with it, her reply was 'It sounds great, even if it is about me'!

But the realisation that other people can do her promotion for her (provided she does a bit first) has made it so much easier for her to grow her business. In fact, her exact words were, 'Networking has given me a business. Before that, it was just a dream.'

Postscript: what happened next

Kate is still a very Unnatural Promoter so her story is still relevant, but some key things have changed since she started Violets Kitchen. For one thing, Amelie is of school age: but the major news is that Kate no longer runs this business. In fact, she's changed her business entirely, and is now offering outsourced marketing services through her new company, Airbourne Business Support.

As Violets Kitchen got more successful, and as Amelie turned from young child into school-age child, Kate found herself baking in the evenings and weekends, impacting on the quality of her family life. There was an option to open up a shop – but that would only have taken her out of Amelie's life even more. Amelie was the reason Kate started the business – she was now the reason it would stop.

Running her outsourced marketing business had been something that she'd had in mind as a plan B for years, but now was the time to make it work – and it allowed Kate to refocus on her why in life. Not only that, but as that business has become more successful, she's now started taking on employees. The two people she's taken on so far have both faced similar challenges to Kate herself, in terms of challenging childbirth and wanting to build a working life that revolves around bringing up young children. Her new business isn't only reinforcing her own Why, it's helping other people with theirs.

Does Kate still do any baking? Yes, she and Amelie do it together: but only for fun!

5 Telling Your Story

Let me tell you about Marie.

Marie is a travel agent, and at a networking event I heard her talk about a recent client in her business. The story went like this:

Marie was sitting in her office one Friday. It was about a quarter to six in the early evening. Like most entrepreneurs, Marie wanted to grow her business – but she was honest enough to say that, right then, she wasn't proactively thinking about bringing new business in. She had been thinking about the weekend, and the Indian takeaway she was having with her friends that evening.

Anyway, the phone rang. It became clear quickly that the woman on the other end of the line was very upset. She was crying, and when Marie asked her what had happened, it turned out that the woman was going to be getting married the next day. She was then going to the Caribbean for her honeymoon on the Sunday.

The Unnatural Promoter

The problem was that she has just heard the honeymoon was off – a local strike had grounded all flights. Her big day was going to be ruined.

You can understand why she would be upset. Marie responded by saying she couldn't promise anything, but wanted to ask one question.

Where would she be the following morning?

The answer came – she would be getting ready for the wedding at her mum's house, and she told Marie the address.

Marie put the phone down, then picked it up again as she called a couple of contacts and got online. She was able to source exactly the same type of holiday: similar quality hotel, dates, transfers, even down to a couple of the activities the couple had planned for their stay. The only difference was that instead of the Caribbean, the couple would be off to Hawaii.

The next morning, Marie went to the lady's mum's house, and hand-delivered the tickets. She told her that she had waived the last-minute booking fee of £150 as a wedding gift, and wished the couple a lovely wedding day and an amazing honeymoon.

Two weeks later, Marie received a card in the post from the newlywed couple. On the front, there was a selfie picture of the couple, with an idyllic Hawaiian beach scene behind them. Inside, there was a short, handwritten message that said: 'Thank you. I don't know what we'd have done without you.'

End of story.

I have a question for you. Would you be prepared to refer business to Marie? Of course you would. The key question is *why*?

Various answers would likely come out. She offered great service. She went the extra mile. She resolved the problem – she was very good at what she does. She was empathetic. She cared. She even offered a discount.

All of these are valid. But I think that there is another, much more important reason why you would refer business to Marie.

It's because I told you a story.

How does telling a story help the Unnatural Promoter?

I had a quick chat with Marie after hearing the story about the honeymoon. It became clear that she was a very Unnatural Promoter, and the thought of having to talk about herself at that meeting filled her with dread.

She was telling me about how she had used to go to networking events, and tried to describe her business to people.

In the end, she would only ever describe it in very generic terms: she could talk about how she offered great service, where she'd booked holidays to recently, how she could match the prices offered by high street travel agents, and how she was on the end of the phone if one of her clients ever needed her.

But it wasn't working. Talking about herself so much and what she could do for her clients, made her feel self-conscious. It got to the point where she didn't want to go networking at all. Added to that, she wasn't getting referrals.

The Unnatural Promoter

She changed tack. To her, it was clear how she'd added value with the honeymoon client, so she started telling that story. She demonstrated social proof of her results.

Immediately, two things happened. She started getting more referrals, particularly for honeymoons. Secondly, she felt more confident to promote herself while networking – so she did it more. This created a virtuous circle: she was doing more networking, while at the same time promoting herself more effectively. Her business skyrocketed.

Not having to talk about herself was huge. But there's more. Why did she get more referrals?

The answer is that we're all human beings, and, simply put, we like stories. When we hear about a situation a fellow human went through, we find ourselves relating to it. We put ourselves in the person's shoes and think about how it would feel if we were in the same situation.

These feelings could come from a whole range of emotions – happiness, sadness, anger, frustration, embarrassment – but when the listener feels the emotion within them, they relate to the story even more. It is this visceral connection that makes stories so effective.

Listeners also just want to know what the ending is. Did everything work out, and did everyone live happily ever after?

In a networking context when you're trying to promote yourself, remember that you are effectively 'competing' with all the other networkers for their attention. Think about the types of conversations you have had when you have been to networking events recently. Were they interesting? Can you recall many of them?

My guess is the answers to those questions is 'no'.

But because people relate to characters in stories, and because they want to know how the story ends, they tend to listen. This particularly happens at a networking event, when we are bombarded by multiple conversations and meeting new people all the time.

Stories will make you stand out, and you will be remembered. Instead of giving people facts about your business, making sweeping comments about how you provide great customer service, or how you can help this person and that company – which everyone else will be doing – you will stand out because you are telling people something that they want to hear.

Not only that, but in the days and weeks afterwards, the conversation is likely to be remembered. If a story has been delivered well, and creates that visceral connection for the listener, then it will be recalled, and – crucially when trying to generate referrals – retold.

That's what needs to happen if referrals are going to be passed on.

The third party who will receive the product or service needs to be prepared to take a call from you, the service provider. It makes it much easier for this to happen if they are told how you have added value to someone else. Stories make it much easier for the person in the middle passing the referral to explain how you will add value and therefore get the target to take the call.

But I'm no good at telling stories...

Many people tell me this. They say something like 'I'm just an accountant' and tell me that surely no one wants to hear about what they do.

And I tell them that they're right. No one wants to hear what an accountant *does*. I'm not just picking on accountants – insert any profession or trade here. We genuinely don't care about what you did. What you did is actually really boring – from a storytelling point of view.

More interesting is what the client who used your services felt. What do they think about you? When you tell the story from the client's point of view, not your own, people will want to listen.

I would argue that there are really three sections to a client-focused story such as the one I told about Marie at the start of this chapter:

1. **Setting the Scene:** this is where you provide the context. Remember – it should be context from the client's point of view. What was happening for them? How were they feeling? What would have happened to them if they carried on without your intervention?

2. **What You Did:** this is where you tell your listener how you solved the situation or problem that the client had.

3. **The Afters:** this is where you tell the story about what happened to the client after you did the work. How do they feel now? How does this compare to how they were feeling before you showed up? What has happened since? Remember – this section should be from the client's point of view! Please also note that

'afters' isn't my word. It comes from Andy Bounds, in his book *The Jelly Effect* (2010). He talks about how we don't buy a product or service; we buy what it gives us *after* we've bought it.

The key to effective storytelling is how much importance you give to each of these three sections. Unfortunately, when networking, most stories you hear will be 100 per cent based in section 2 – what you did.

This means that stories do get boring, because we have to listen to how the accountant saved some tax (sorry accountants, I know I'm at it again...). But it's the same with whatever industry you are in – no one cares about what you did in terms of the story.

It is much better to base the vast majority of your story in sections 1 and 3. This is where you share the story from the client's point of view – how they felt before, how they feel now, and so on. Of course, you may well need to reference what you did – but the weighting and importance of the three sections should be something like this:

1. Setting the Scene: 45%
2. What You Did: 10%
3. The Afters: 45%

Essentially, sections 1 and 3 have roughly even importance in terms of the story. Of course, every story is different. In some cases, it might be necessary to spend more time on the set-up – while for another story, it might be more important to give more focus on the afters. Just make sure that you don't spend time in section 2.

The ingredients of a great story

Just as when you follow a recipe when baking a cake, there are various ingredients needed to make a story.

A problem

If there isn't an issue or problem – then there isn't a story. Think about the last film you saw, or book you read. Did everything start off with everyone being happy, and then the story went on and everyone remained happy, and then it finished, and all the characters were still happy? Of course not! They may have started off okay, but then the world exploded/they fell out/something conspired against them to make their life difficult.

The point here is clear – there must be something wrong, or there won't be a story to tell. But there's another benefit to focusing on the problem: it fixes the story in the context of the client, keeping it firmly in section 1, Setting the Scene.

A resolution

If there's a problem, then the story should tell us what the resolution was. Given you're talking about client success stories, it is important that you show off your abilities/customer service/value by making the client's problem go away.

Note that not every story will have a happy ending, and sometimes they are more powerful when they don't – but there will still be a resolution to the problem.

Making sure the resolution is a key part of the story ensures that you focus it on the client, pushing the story into section 3, The Afters.

Characters

It is useful to look at the characters in terms of the classical hero and villain structure. In this type of story, you are the hero! You might not be focusing much on what you specifically did, but you are the one that has solved the problem for the client such that they are now saving money/more efficient/living a better life.

The villain is not usually an actual villain like in the movies. Often it is a metaphorical villain, represented by the problem or issue the client is facing.

And of course, if you have a hero and a villain, the other character you usually see is the victim role. This is your client, who is suffering because of the metaphorical villain, and then you, the hero, swoop in to save the day. In these stories, we need to focus on the victim's part of the story more than anyone else.

Details

Think back to Marie's story for a moment. When did the phone call come to Marie's office? That's right, a quarter to six on a Friday evening, when she was just starting to think about the curry she was looking forward to with her family.

It's these small details – largely irrelevant to the rest of the story – that help anchor the story in our minds because they help put the listener in the shoes of the protagonist. Listeners know what it's like to be thinking about the weekend on a Friday afternoon and about the Indian takeaway they've promised themselves.

So, while they aren't important to the rest of the story, the context they provide, along with making it easier to recall the story later, makes them vital. A quick note here though – just put in one or two details. A story can become clunky and overly long if there are too many details.

Fact

It should go without saying that the stories you tell to get referrals must be true. You will get found out very quickly if they aren't!

That said, it is necessary to make the most of the key bits of the story. When you talk about the client's issue – dig further to demonstrate the true implications of their situation. I heard a payroll specialist tell a story once about a new client who had previously been given advice about how to handle their company's payroll. That advice, while well intended at the time, was now unlawful, and the client had absolutely no idea that they were breaking the law.

The logical conclusion then was that if the payroll specialist didn't advise them on a new, legal scheme, the client could potentially have gone to jail. I encouraged the payroll specialist to focus on this in his story. In the end, his 'hero' work was to keep the client out of jail.

Emotion

Last on the list, but by far the most important in terms of telling stories from the client's point of view. When we hear the word 'emotion', often the first thought that comes to mind is sadness. But emotion covers such a wide range of feelings: happiness, anger, frustration, worry, joy, sadness, anticipation, surprise, disgust.

All emotions can make a story powerful. When listeners hear what the victim character is going through, they connect what they're hearing with their own experiences. It's this connection that makes the story work, and the more visceral and real it feels to them, the better.

So, when you talk about what was happening to the client before you (the superhero) came along, really think about what emotion they were feeling at that time. And then, once you've done your bit, the fact that you've turned that usually negative emotion into such a positive one makes your story even more powerful.

Getting your story told

Hopefully you've now seen how you can shout about what you've achieved with at least some level of confidence and demonstrate social proof of how good you are. Because you're not talking about what you did, and instead placing the emphasis on how the client felt you are a) not feeling like you're bragging, making it more likely you will actually shout about yourself, but also b) being more interesting.

But it still would be good if you didn't have to do that, wouldn't it? What if there was a way to promote yourself and your business, and someone else did the work for you... Well there is: receiving testimonials and recommendations from your clients.

Getting your clients to write down what difference you've made to them is such a powerful way to promote yourself because it is the ultimate in social proof. Everyone needs to be reminded of positive achievements sometimes, especially as an Unnatural Promoter – and I sometimes just browse through the recommendations I've received on LinkedIn. It makes me remember the positivity from the time with the client, which of course feels nice: but it also gives me the belief I need from time to time to promote myself more effectively.

Two key things come from a well-written client testimonial. Firstly, there are the benefits of someone else saying it, in the same way that we take far more notice of customer reviews than adverts written by the company themselves. Secondly, because the customer has written it, it automatically will be put from their point of view, which satisfies the key point from the last few pages.

The best way to get testimonials is to ask for them. As soon as you've finished a piece of work for a client – ask! Assuming it has gone well (and of course it did, it was you, the superhero...), they will have gone through some form of transformative effect where you either took away their need or worry or made a positive difference.

Yes, as an Unnatural Promoter, you need to get over the awkward feeling asking for something. But the powerful benefits of being able to display credibility-enhancing comments about how good you are from independent businesses outweigh the worry of feeling like you're being pushy.

By far the best place to ask for client testimonials is via LinkedIn. The platform has a built-in feature where you can ask for recommendations:

If that request comes to someone just after you've done a good piece of work for them, they are very likely to do it for you. I always find that it is a good idea to ask them verbally before you send it. The notification from LinkedIn then has a simple confirmatory feel to it.

Consider also asking for more than just a testimonial. Ask specific questions about your product or service that mean the client will have to write down how you have benefited them. The sorts of questions you might ask are:

➤ What benefits have you seen since you started using our service?

➤ How much time have you saved since we started working together?

➤ How much money did our product save you?

Other forms of testimonial do exist: in BNI, one of the key contributions that members make to their group is writing up a testimonial for another member on how they added value. They are then encouraged to print it out on letterheaded paper, copy and paste the text to LinkedIn, and even frame it. Think about how you'd feel if not only had a client written some lovely words about you, but they'd taken the time to get it framed. That means it is more likely to get displayed on their office wall.

If possible, ask for testimonials on video. They will be harder to get, because not everyone is going to feel comfortable to do it – but the personal feeling and authenticity will shine through far more than via written text.

Using your testimonials

Once you've got the testimonial from your client, you've got to use it! Again, this can go against the grain for the Unnatural Promoter, because it feels like you are bragging. But remember, your potential future clients are looking for reasons why they should use you.

How can you use testimonials?

➤ Take quotes from testimonials and display them on your website's homepage – the more prominent the better

➤ Use the quotes on printed materials –

brochures, banners, etc.

➤ Add them to a 'what our clients say about us' page on your website

➤ Share them on social media

➤ Add them into blog content

➤ Display framed testimonials in your workspace

➤ If you have a waiting area in your business, compile a file of all the testimonials you've received so potential customers browse through them

➤ Use them in email marketing campaigns

Do you want to get more testimonials?

Of course you do!

The best way to get more testimonials is to give them. If you write nice words about people – they are likely to reciprocate. At the very least, it will make them more open to you asking.

If doesn't matter if you are the service provider or the client – just be open about your positive working relationship with the other party, and they will appreciate it.

Chapter 5: Action Steps

➤ Start writing up stories about how you helped some recent clients. It is worth doing this for a few of your clients – the best one will become apparent, but all the stories will be worthwhile to tell networking contacts.

➤ Work on the best story in more detail. Really consider the position the client was in before you started with them. Talk to the client and ask them. Then keep asking the question – what would that have meant for them if the situation had continued?

➤ Also ask the client what they think of you now. What difference is there now? Have you saved them time/money/effort? Have you made a profound difference to their life?

➤ Practise delivering this best client story, then use it in conversations when networking.

➤ Ask your clients for recommendations and testimonials. Start by asking them verbally, then sending them a LinkedIn recommendation request.

➤ Write testimonials and recommendations for your contacts – they may well reciprocate!

Case Study 2
Promoting Myself...

This is a picture of my dad, Martin Lawson. It was taken about three-and-a-half weeks before he died. You'll note that he has an oxygen tube to his nose – this was because he suffered from cystic fibrosis (CF), a disease that clogs up the lungs, making breathing difficult, before finally making it impossible.

You may be thinking that he looks quite old for a CF sufferer, and you'd be right. He was 69 when he died, whereas most patients with the disease are young. Typical life expectancy has increased to about 40 years old, but my dad had a slightly different strain of CF. In fact, he was only diagnosed with CF when he was in his early 60s, although throughout his life he had problems with his lungs.

Every single day, he spent an hour lying on his back coughing up the phlegm and mucus in his lungs. As a family, we'd go for walking holidays to places like the Lake District. Dad would always bring up the rear, stopping regularly for breath.

When he died, I decided to do something to honour his memory and raise funds for CF. Apparently a cure will be found – it's just a question of money and time. However, time isn't something that 70,000 worldwide sufferers of CF have.

Running a marathon had been on my bucket list for as long as I can remember. The only problem is, to tick it off the list, you actually have to run it...

But I now had the perfect opportunity: I could do it in honour of my dad, while at the same time raising money for a great cause. Which marathon? Well, I've lived in London my entire life, so it could only be the London Marathon.

Why am I sharing this story? Well, for an Unnatural Promoter, I was about to have to step far outside my comfort zone. Forget the running, I needed to promote myself more than I had ever done before! During the process, I learned seven lessons that might help other Unnatural Promoters.

Lesson 1: Start with Why

Whatever you want to do – if you don't start with why you want to achieve the goal, it makes it a lot harder. If not impossible.

Two things helped me. Firstly, it gave me something to motivate me when it got hard. As if the fundraising I needed to do wasn't enough, I still had to think about running a marathon. I know you know this, but 26.2 miles is a long way!

Secondly, it meant that my contacts, who I needed to sponsor me, bought in to my challenge. Whether or not they knew my dad, it was clear why I was doing what I was doing.

Lesson 2: Aim high

What I really needed though was buy-in.

In life we all have role models, and my dad was one for me. He was an extraordinarily high achiever, and if I can do half the things he did in his life I'll be happy. As such, I wanted to set myself some high goals – both for the fundraising and my running time.

Even getting a place in the London Marathon can be tough, but because of my dad's story, the CF Trust were happy to give me a place. I clearly remember the conversation I had with their fundraising team.

'We're very happy to give you a place, but you know you must commit to raising £1,500, don't you?'

With my plans, that wasn't going to be a problem. But I wanted much more than that. Was it going to be £3,000?

£5,000? £10,000? In the end, I went a little bit crazy, and decided to try and raise £26,385 (a marathon is 26 miles, 385 yards).

I should remind you that this was my first marathon. I'd done a few 5km runs, but nothing like this. Again, I set myself a ridiculous goal: instead of just running the marathon, my aim was less than 3½ hours. Accepted, it's not world record pace – but trust me when I say it was a big ask.

I had my goals: £26,385, and sub-3½ hours. I didn't realise it then, but the fact that I had set such high targets was crucial for buy-in. I needed people to be interested to feel comfortable talking about it.

Lesson 3: Tell everyone

As an Unnatural Promoter, you might imagine that this was the hardest part. And you'd be right! When actually running, that was my 'me time', relaxing from pressures of work and family life.

But the fundraising goal required me to tell people what I was doing. If I didn't – they wouldn't sponsor me.

I decided that I would use the opportunity of speaking to a large audience to do this. I was lucky in that in my BNI role, I had that opportunity at a conference about 10 months before the race. You can make out my goals behind me on the slide:

There were two benefits. Firstly, as someone shouted out from the audience, I wanted their sponsorship money.

But the second was that by going public with my goals, I had bought myself accountability. People would ask me – how's the fundraising going? Are you going to hit your targets? I couldn't escape it.

I became very focused. A little later in my training, I suffered an injury when I tore a muscle in my calf. The physio told me:

> 'I'll get you to the start line, but you'll have to forget about your 3½-hour target.'

> 'Er no,' I replied. 'I don't think you understand – I must hit my goal.'

We agreed to disagree – I couldn't let people down once I'd told them what I was doing.

Lesson 4: Use your network

You might think that given my position in BNI, it was my network that helped me to reach the fundraising goal. However I took something else from how to use my network.

When learning a new skill, you need help. There were four key people who helped me:

1. Ed, my running coach. A ridiculously good runner who set my training plans, and got my muscle strength and conditioning right (which hadn't even occurred to me...)

2. Liv, my sponsorship and fundraising expert. As an Unnatural Promoter, I was going to need a lot of help here.

3. Ray, my physio. While we disagreed on my 3½-hour target, he did an amazing job with my calf.

4. Tim, my race day guide. With 50,000 runners, a lot can go wrong!

What got me is how I know these people. Liv is my sister. Tim is my business partner. Liv introduced me to Ed. And Tim introduced me to Ray.

I needed to get specialist advice – but the people I turned to were very close to me. And they were able to introduce me to the others.

Lesson 5: Get expert advice

Much as I'd love to describe the running training I did (hill repeats anyone?), the focus here must be the fundraising.

Liv was my expert for two reasons. Firstly, she had run the London Marathon, so she had first-hand experience. More importantly though, she does communications for a living.

She taught me that my cause wasn't important to people. I don't mean that they didn't care – many of them knew my dad, or it was easy to get them to buy in when they heard the story.

But sponsoring me wasn't their *priority*. Everyone has their own stuff going on, and while they do mean it when they say they'll sponsor you, it's a question of priorities as to whether they will actually do it.

Liv wrote my extensive fundraising plan. This included emails, written to encourage sponsorship, and to thank and ask for 'referrals' to other potential sponsors. It included pre-scripted and ad hoc social media posts: these made me feel uncomfortable – but having someone else write them made it easier.

The last part was regular Facebook Live videos, taken just after a run. These, combined with me telling everyone my goals, made a massive difference because I built up a following. People wanted to hear where I was up to, which meant they tuned in.

Lesson 6: It will get tough

Whatever your goal – it will be difficult. If it were easy, everyone would do it.

Pounding the streets on training runs is tough. Pushing myself to record another Facebook Live, or send another round of fundraising emails was difficult. Even with excellent training, there will come a point (around 22 miles) where it hurts.

That is where I circled back to Lesson 1 – my Why. Picturing my dad and drawing inspiration from asking myself 'What would he have done?' made the difference.

Lesson 7: You'll do better than you would have done, even if you fail

So, the big question – how did I do?

Unfortunately, I didn't hit my running goal – I completed the 2017 London Marathon in 3 hours, 32 minutes and 54 seconds.

I beat myself up about not hitting it, but as Tim, my race day expert, puts it: only one per cent of the world's population will ever run a marathon, and on my very first one, my time put me in the top 20 per cent of marathon runners. And that's not too bad.

The fundraising? I can still scarcely believe what happened. Having set myself a target of £26,385, which felt so scary and far away, I raised £40,688.40. I beat it by over 50 per cent!

That's where I take the biggest learning – and it's something that will help Unnatural Promoters be more confident in shouting about themselves.

I could have set my goal to 'complete the marathon', or to run it in 4 hours. Even though I failed, I still went faster than if I'd set a goal of 4 hours. I could have set a goal to raise £5,000 – and even if I did 50 per cent better again, I'd have raised only £7,500.

When your Why is strong, and you set ridiculous goals, people will buy into you more. You won't need to shout about yourself so much, because they'll be so blown away by what you're doing that they'll want to help you anyway.

I just hope I made my dad proud. Love you, Dad – I'll miss you forever.

6 Defining Your Target Market

The less time you have to spend time promoting yourself, the better. You don't want to broadcast about your business repeatedly. Even accepting that you are not going to do all the promoting yourself, it still makes you feel uncomfortable.

But time spent promoting and networking has to get good results. The world is a big place. How do you know that the people you're building relationships with are going to introduce you to the right potential clients? Isn't it a bit a scattergun?

The short answer to this is yes, it is, there's no knowing who you are going to get introduced to. That is one of the joys of networking – you don't know who other people know and how they could help you.

But there is a better way to promote yourself – knowing your target market. The more specific you are about who you want to speak to, the more likely you are to get referrals to them.

Getting specific

This sounds counterintuitive. You might think that ignoring a whole swathe of potential customers to focus on one specific target is ridiculous: you wouldn't be the first. Go to any networking event, and listen to what people say when trying to get referrals:

> ➤ 'I help people save money on their phone bills, so a good referral for me is **somebody** with a mobile phone.'

> ➤ 'As an accountant, a good referral for me is **everybody** that wants their business to be more profitable.'

> ➤ 'I clean cars, so a good referral for me is **anybody** with a car.'

In all three of these examples the business owner is being too general. Who do you know who has a mobile phone, wants a more profitable business, or has a car? Everyone.

But does this make it easier to refer them? Unfortunately not. Using the words anybody, everybody, somebody tends to lead to nobody. Let me give you an example.

I'd heard John say 'a good referral for me is anyone with a car' many times. He runs a car-cleaning business – but not your average car-cleaning business. He focuses on detailing high-end cars: Ferraris, Rolls Royces and so on. Owners of cars like these want them kept in pristine condition – car-cleaning to a whole new level.

John wasn't getting referrals. The issue was he was asking for anyone with a car. However, because he wanted high-end cars, his prices reflected this. This meant that while he *could* cater for customers with a standard car, people like this didn't want or need high-end service, so business was slow. He thought he was making it easier to pass him a referral because he was including anyone.

I asked John about his best recent customer. He'd just cleaned a red Ferrari – so I suggested the next time he went networking, he shouldn't ask for anyone with a car: ask to be referred to a red Ferrari owner. He looked unsure, but I encouraged him to use those exact words.

Guess what? Someone in his network had a friend with a red Ferrari. An introduction was made, and John had a new client.

The story doesn't end there. It turned out that John's new client was in the Ferrari Owners' Club of Scotland – and referred John on to other members. Now he was cleaning and detailing lots of Ferraris. Owners of Ferraris also have other high-end cars – so he got more Lamborghinis, McLarens and so on.

All of that came from a change of language. He thought he was trying to be helpful to his network by asking for 'anyone with a car' – but he wasn't. He had good relationships. This meant people *wanted* to help him – but he wasn't giving them the tools to do so.

Your network will be the same. You've built good relationships, so your network will be happy to promote you, and want to do so. So what's the red Ferrari in your business?

The change of focus also allowed John to get the business he really wanted. This allowed him to build a better business. Promoting your business effectively isn't just about getting new clients: it's also about improving the quality of your clients.

Full service or niche?

Plenty of businesses proudly describe themselves as 'one-stop shops', covering all your given needs in a sector. The challenge in a modern internet-based world is that it is so easy for consumers to source specific suppliers and to compare prices at the touch of a button.

It's a similar challenge when promoting your business when networking. You might offer a full service in your sector, but that doesn't help generate referrals for you.

Here's an example I heard recently: a web designer was presenting his business, and said: 'I offer a full service for creating your website, but everyone knows what a web designer does, so I won't bore you with that.'

As he carried on talking, my mind drifted from what he was saying. I can't remember anything else he said, because I started thinking what a web designer *actually does*. I mean, I know they create websites – but to a non-techie like me, that's about it!

Websites can have lots of pages or few pages, you can buy products/services on some websites but not on others, you can interact with some websites but not others, some sites link to applications, some look better on mobile devices – the list goes on. And that's without considering the design, copywriting, pictures and video.

All these areas require certain specialisms and – while I'm not suggesting that a web designer should only cover one of these areas in their business – when promoting their business through networking, they should chunk it down.

If they do this, then it is much clearer for networking contacts to help them. They don't need the detail or the jargon, just the tools to pass the web designer a referral.

For example, their focus might be small, five-page websites for a start-up. In this case, they'd want networking contacts thinking about people they knew who were starting up a new business, and the web designer could tell them what to say accordingly.

Or, they may focus on mobile-friendly websites – in which case their networking message would be to look for websites that are fine on a desktop but terrible on a mobile.

Another big benefit can come from avoiding the full-service approach. Sometimes you hear people say that they don't want to go networking because they meet too many competitors. They are after the same clients!

But, using web design again, what if you focused on small five-page websites for new businesses, and you met another web designer who built larger, e-commerce websites for established businesses? By being targeted, you don't compete at all.

Building a relationship together could then lead to all sorts of referral possibilities. If the small web designer was asked to build a large e-commerce site, they could refer the other company, safe in the knowledge that they would provide a better service than they could. Likewise, the bigger web designer would feel comfortable that they weren't wasting time with the 'wrong' sort of clients.

Getting specific – how can I be more targeted when promoting myself?

This is where so many businesspeople get stuck. They understand why targeting their networking efforts can work, but they don't know how to do it. Let me help. There is a simple question you can ask yourself that will, in virtually every case, help you be specific.

Think back to John and the red Ferrari. I simply asked him who was a good current client. So, in your business – who is the best current or recent client? Then ask yourself: if you could get referrals to more clients like that, would that be good? I'm going to assume the answer would be yes.

So – you've got to ask for them. This works in two different ways, depending on whether you sell to other businesses (i.e. you are a business-to-business operator), or you sell your product/service to the general public (business-to-consumer).

Business to business

Let's take an example where a good current client is a firm of accountants. All we do then is pick another firm of accountants. You could ask yourself the following questions:

1. **Where do I want the accountants to be based?**
    Getting other people to promote you should lead to better-quality business. There's no sense asking for companies that are based miles away when you only want referrals to people in your locality. Equally, you may be targeting national or international clients.

2. **Which firm of accountants do I want to ask for?**
Just pick one! Name the firm of accountants you'd like to be referred to. It might be you know of a suitable target, but if you don't, just Google it. Search for accounting companies in a given location. Check their websites to see what sort of size practice they are, what they specialise in, and where they are based. Then pick one.

3. **What job title/level do I need?** Once you know the company, think about the person you need to speak to. If it is a small business, then it might be the owner. In larger businesses, maybe the CEO isn't necessary, and the head of HR or finance would be more appropriate. Sticking with accountants though, we'll assume that we need to speak to the managing partner.

4. **What is the person's name?** You might think that this isn't necessary, but I would encourage you to always find the name of the person you'd like to be referred to. Why? Because referrals come from relationships. We might be doing this for business, but one of your contacts is hopefully going to know the person you are targeting. It may be a work relationship, but it might come because they're mates. Or neighbours. Or their kids go to the same school.

It is often a personal relationship that gets you an introduction, so if you didn't mention the person's name, you immediately reduce the likelihood of getting the referral.

So how do you find out the person's name? Do some research – a quick check on LinkedIn/Google/the company's website will give you the answer 99 per cent of the time.

The Unnatural Promoter

We have now got all the ingredients to be specific. A good referral for me would be *Adam Loveday, Managing Partner* of *Murray Accountants*, based in *Chester*.

And that is all. It really is that simple. My experience here tends to throw up two challenges.

Challenge 1

People get stuck because their mindset is 'Why would this company want to talk to me?' They are approaching thinking they've got to cold call the company. Remember: you will be *referred* by someone who has a vested interest in helping you. Someone in your network is going to promote you and your service so the target *wants* to talk to you.

Challenge 2

I accept that people reading this may still be thinking that this is counterintuitive. If you ask to speak to *Adam Loveday* of *Murray Accountants*, are you not cutting out all other accountants, and indeed anyone else who might need your service?

Two things tend to happen when business owners are specific. Firstly, while the chance of people actually knowing *Adam Loveday* is small, there is a much greater chance that they have a connection to *Murray Accountants*. Maybe they know someone else who works there, or they have a client who's done work for the company. All you need right now is an in – that person might then be able to connect us on to *Adam Loveday*.

I used to support a BNI group in Hertfordshire, and every time I visited, I would write down specific referral requests that the businesses were asking for. I would then send an email to the ten people who work in the office, asking if anyone had any connection to these people or the companies they work for. How many times did I get a positive response? Every single time! I didn't create an actual referral every time, but there was always someone in the office with some sort of connection to the targets.

The second thing that tends to happen is your network might not know anyone in the firm you are targeting, but they play golf with the managing partner at *Curtis & Sutton* accountants. The chances are that would be a good introduction for you.

Remember that you are giving your network the tools to promote you and get you referrals. The more you help them by giving them clues of the clients you want, the better. It will give them more to go on. And remember: they *want* to help you.

Business to consumer

If you sell your products to the general public, then you can't ask for an individual person. It doesn't offer the same possibilities that naming someone in a company does.

It wouldn't tell the listener anything about them, so they can't then think about other people similar to them. It would also potentially break client confidentiality to name people you want to speak to.

But, as already seen, if you are asking *anyone* with a car, or *everyone* with a mobile phone, you are not going to be giving your network the tools to promote you effectively.

So there are various ways to be more specific when targeting consumers, principally about defining the demographics of who you are looking to do business with. As with business to business, think of a good current client. Then consider:

> **What stage of life are they at?** Are they young or old? Are they married? Are they about to get married? Are they on their second marriage? Do they have children? Are their children young? Have their children left home? Are they drawing a pension?

> **Do they work?** Where do they work? Are they in a profession, such as a doctor? Do they run their own business?

> **Are they homeowners?** Or do they rent? A small house? Or a big house, with a driveway or a swimming pool?

> **Do they have a car?** Do they have two or more cars in the family? Do they have a certain type of car?

> **Where do they live?** As well as it being easier for you to service potential clients, where they live within a given locality can give you clues to your network about the type of person they are. Anyone who lives in that area will know that one side of town, or even a given road, is more affluent.

All these questions (and there will be more besides) will put a picture of your ideal client in the minds of your network. Instead of anyone/everyone/someone – they will now be thinking of real people that they could refer.

That said though, you can do even better.

End user or introducer?

For business-to-consumer businesses, we have only roughly segmented the population. Let's say a good current client is in their 50s, they are approaching retirement, they have grown-up children, and they tend to have relatively large houses because they need lots of space when the grandkids are over.

While some referral possibilities will come from that information alone, many more referrals can come if we don't target the end user directly.

Instead, think about who could introduce us to a person like that? In this case, a financial advisor might be a good start. Approaching retirement, they may have been seeking advice on their finances. Equally, they live in a nice house, so an estate agent may be a good connection. Focusing on their interests, golf courses might be a good way in.

The key is to think of people who will likely know a good number of end users in your target market. Then ask for referrals to them instead. There are two benefits of doing this.

Firstly, it becomes a lot easier to be specific. If you decide that estate agents were the best approach, you've then just got to ask for one. It's back to business to business – pick which estate agent, which job title you need to speak to (i.e. the sales manager perhaps) and do some research to get their name.

Secondly, there is the referral potential that comes from promoting yourself in this way. When you go for the end user, you've only got one potential client. When you ask for an introducer, how many referrals to end users could they give you? Two? Ten? A hundred? Going for introducers also works for business-to-business operators too.

The Unnatural Promoter

The key thing to remember is that it will never be a short-term strategy. You can't expect to get a referral to the estate agent, and for them to immediately start giving you referrals to people with big houses.

But, if you take time to build a relationship with them, and try to help them and give them referrals, at some point the estate agent is going to ask how they can help you. Then you can say 'Oh, it's funny you should ask...'

Chapter 6: Action Steps

- ➤ Think about networking you've done. Have you ever used the words 'anybody', 'everybody' or 'somebody' when describing the referrals you are looking for?

- ➤ Consider what the 'red Ferrari' in your business is.

- ➤ Make it easier for your referral partners to promote you by chunking down your business into smaller parts. Then pick one area at a time and focus on asking for those types of referrals when networking.

- ➤ Produce a list of ten target referrals to educate your network who you'd like to do business with. Start off by thinking of a good current client. Then do some research to pick companies and the names of the people that you need to speak to.

- ➤ If you sell your product to consumers, note down the demographics of your ideal customer so you can educate your network better on how to find your business.

- ➤ Think about who would be a good introducer for you. Ask your network to introduce you to these people, then build a relationship with them so they are minded to help you.

7 Building Relationships One at a Time

I have never been a big fan of going to events. Whether a big or small event, I need to pluck up the courage to go and talk to people. Of course, I know I *can* physically do it, and once I get into conversation, I'll be okay – but I don't enjoy it.

One of the biggest networking falsehoods is the belief that the only way to network is to go to big events. The day I realised this was a very good day. It was in April 2005.

I was attending my first 'proper' conference. There were 300 people there, and of course I was very nervous. It was very warm – one of those spring days where it feels like summer has arrived. As such, during the breaks, everyone went outside to enjoy the sunshine.

But what specifically got my attention was that the conference organisers had designated the breaks as time for one-to-ones. At most events, attendees will grab a coffee and then chat with whoever is nearby. That, or they will be off 'checking their emails', trying to pretend that they're busy when in fact they'd love to be talking to someone. Yes, I have done that plenty of times...

At this conference, however, the MC encouraged everyone to find a partner while the delegates were still sitting in their seats. Then, they would find a suitable place to have a conversation. Some people had even set meetings up prior to the conference.

For anyone lacking confidence, this was so much better! Everyone just turned to the people around them, and without exception, found themselves with a partner. Much better than hanging around hoping to get into a conversation.

But not only did setting up one-to-one conversations make life easier, it meant that better networking was done.

Networking is simply about talking to people and building relationships – it stands to reason that having a one-on-one conversation will be better than mixing with many people at an event. Let's look at some of the reasons why:

You're less likely to be interrupted. At an event, whether large or small, there are always going to be other people there. So, if you get into an interesting conversation or arrange to meet someone there, other people will come and join in. The whole point of attending a networking event is, after all, to meet people. In a one-on-one conversation, this won't happen.

It is easier to hear what people are saying. With the noise and hubbub of a networking event, it can be hard to have a proper conversation. Lots of other people around, having to lean in close to hear someone well enough, doesn't make networking easy. Having a one-on-one chat is much easier: you're in a setting that suits an easy two-way conversation.

The conversation will only be more meaningful. At an event, the likely interruptions, the potential difficulty hearing your partner, and the fact you are likely to have only a few minutes talking to each other means the conversation will only ever go so far. To build a stronger relationship requires taking the time to converse on a one-to-one basis.

Sit down and relax! If we want to have a conversation where we're going to build a relationship on a deeper level, then standing up in a crowded room is never going to be ideal. It's surely better to sit down in a couple of comfortable chairs while having a chat.

Make it easier to write notes or share examples. Again, we are looking to build a relationship that leads to something. That means we will likely need to take notes, or perhaps show examples/pictures on an electronic device. This is much easier when sitting down comfortably.

Why one-to-ones work well for an Unnatural Promoter

So, one-to-ones are a better way to network. Crucially, they allow you to build stronger relationships – and that is what counts when it comes to getting your contacts to promote you.

There are also some key points why, as an Unnatural Promoter, one-to-ones will be more effective.

1. As we've already seen, being an Unnatural Promoter means you won't feel particularly comfortable shouting about yourself. Having to attend networking events doesn't help here – because while getting other people to promote you is easier than doing it yourself, you still have to promote yourself to the people you meet.

   Instead, think about having a one-to-one conversation. You are enjoying your preferred beverage. You are in comfortable surroundings. You are chatting with someone you have either already met, or perhaps you know them relatively well. This means there aren't any networking nerves about who to talk to and small talk to keep the conversation going. It's easy.

2. Networking on a one-to-one basis doesn't have to be with someone you're only just getting to know. It could be with a client who you've done business with for years, or an old friend that you are catching up with. To so many people, the word networking freaks them out because they think it is meeting new people – but strengthening existing relationships is just as important.

So don't worry about promoting yourself. If you know your one-to-one partner well, they will likely want to help you, and be more than happy to promote you and your business if they can. Again, this makes promoting yourself very easy.

3. If you are catching up with someone you know well, then what will you likely be talking about? Because you have shared experiences over time, you will probably spend half the time laughing and having fun!

   Aren't we supposed to be doing business and being serious here? Forget that – life has got to be fun; otherwise what's the point?

4. So far we've been self-focused: but what about when you help someone else? Helping your one-to-one partner will make it more likely they will help you. Whether anything comes back or not, how does it feel to help someone? It gives you a warm feeling inside – which makes the one-to-one even more enjoyable. Yes, you can help someone at an event – but it's much easier to do it when one-on-one.

5. Why do you want to get others to promote you? That's right, you want to get referrals, and building relationships on a one-to-one basis is fundamental to making this happen.

   One-to-ones are the best way to have the conversations required to pass referrals back and forth. You'll need to know your networking partners well enough to find them referrals – and vice versa. But there's more than that. You need to educate them about what a good referral is for you. You need to show them how to approach referral targets. That conversation will never happen well enough at a large-scale networking event to be successful.

The three types of one-to-one

There are three different types of one-to-ones, and the appropriate one with a given person will depend on how well you know them.

1. Getting to Know You

As its title suggests, this is about getting to know the other person. You may have met them initially at a networking event, or online – but now it's time to meet face to face.

You're not focusing on referrals yet – you don't know the other person well enough to ask about these on anything more than a superficial basis. Instead, you need to know what sort of person they are, what drives them, and what they want to achieve.

A great way to do this is to base your conversation around these 4 Key Questions:

- ➤ **Where do they want to get to?**
  This is where you find out about their goals and dreams, both in business and personally.
- ➤ **How good are they?**
  What are they good at? How do they add value? What are they proud of?
- ➤ **What are they into?**
  Outside business, what do they enjoy doing?

> **Who do they know?**
> Who are they connected to? Who's in their network? What groups of people do they hang out with?

I'd like to focus on *why* these are good questions. Remember, we are trying to build a referral relationship, so all the questions have meaning in terms of wanting to encourage referrals both back and forward.

Where do they want to get to? If you know the other person's goals, what can you do? Help them to achieve them! How strong will your relationship with someone be (and how much is potentially going to come back to you) if you have made a positive difference to them hitting their life or business goals?

How good are they? Referral generation is really solving a problem for someone, so knowing how your contacts can help will make you a great referral source for your network. But more than that, it is about credibility. Will they enhance your reputation when you pass them a referral to help a friend/client, or will it be a risk? You need to know how good they are if referrals are going to be a part of your relationship.

What are they into? There are two reasons to want to know their interests. Firstly, you will find out any common ground. This is great for relationship development because you'll have interesting things to talk about. Secondly, it enables you to thank the other person when they pass you a referral. Someone I've got to know through networking, Ashley, didn't thank me with a generic gift like a bottle of wine after passing him a referral: no, seeing as we are both into cars, he lent me one of his cars for the weekend!

Who do they know? This one is important because it helps with referral generation. Does the other person know people in my target market? Can I introduce them to people they want to meet?

A good idea to prepare for a Getting to Know You one-to-one is to prepare these questions prior to your meeting – send them on email so they can read them beforehand. They will then either send something over to you before the meeting, or at least have thought about what you will ask them when you meet.

I was reminded of this at a recent Getting to Know You one-to-one I had. It was with Lucinda, a delegate at an event I attended. She had emailed me beforehand, asking if we could have a coffee when we were there.

What impressed me about Lucinda was how prepared she was. The event we met at was being held on a Monday, and the previous week, I had been in the US on a business trip. When I accepted her invitation, I immediately received a typed-up profile with answers to the questions, including images and presented on her company's branding.

I was caught out! I didn't have anything that looked so professional, and being away, I couldn't just send it to her there and then.

Her approach was perfect: by giving me the information beforehand, I could read it through and 'get to know her' before we even met up. In terms of the Visibility, Credibility, Profitability process, she'd pushed ahead with Visibility before we even met.

In fact, she did such a good job, she'd even started to demonstrate her Credibility. This made the Getting to Know You one-to-one far more successful – because I was already thinking about how I could promote her and pass her referrals.

2. Business Builder

Now, the relationship has already been built. It doesn't matter whether that is after a meeting or two, or you have known each other well over a long period of time. The key is you have a relationship.

The dynamic has now changed. Because you know each other, you want to help each other – you both just need the tools to do so. If you are going to help one of your networking contacts to promote them, you need to know who they want to speak to, and how they are going to help that person.

I recall a one-to-one I had several years ago with a mate, Jim. We'd known each other for a while, having initially bonded as we discovered we'd both been students at the University of Birmingham at the same time. Over a drink, Jim was telling me who he wanted introductions to, and one of them was another friend of mine who ran a marketing business locally.

Setting up the introduction was easy – but what made us laugh was that he told me he'd been after this marketing company for ages. Why hadn't I told Jim that I could help him? Because I never knew!

Your networking contacts, if they have a relationship with you, *want to help you*. They just need to know who to promote you to.

There are three major areas to discuss in a Business Builder one-to-one:

> ➤ Tell a story (or stories) about how you helped a recent client (as per the discussion in Chapter 5). This is crucial, because they need this information to do something about the second area.

> ➤ Who do you, specifically, want a referral to? As I found out with Jim, if you don't know who they want to speak to, how on earth are you going to anything about it? We covered this in Chapter 6.

> ➤ How should they introduce you to a potential target client? This is important, as the third party won't necessarily be looking for a new supplier of whatever it is you offer. The success stories will be a good start here.

Remember, if you are going give this information to your partner so they can help you, you'll need to get the same back from them. Encourage them to tell stories about how they've helped their clients, who their targets are, and how best to introduce them.

3. 'Let's just get on with it'

When I wrote *The Unnatural Networker*, I couldn't come up with a better, catchier name than this – and I still haven't. So, let's stick with it, because it does exactly what it says on the tin.

This third sort of one-to-one meeting is only practical once there is a strong relationship between the two parties, as it requires being prepared to pick up the phone and create referrals then and there in the meeting.

The information that you need to share is like the Business Builder one-to-one: who is your target, and what can the other person say to promote you to them so they want to have a conversation with you? Again, you will need a story about how you have helped someone else in a similar situation.

As well as comparing lists of target clients, also share your own contacts and current clients list, so that your partner can see if there is anyone they would like an introduction to.

Then, the only difference is that instead of taking notes and actioning them later, you would then pick up the phone and try to proactively make referrals happen there and then.

Note this is an advanced promotion technique: build up slowly by practising the Getting to Know You and Business Builder one-to-ones first. But if you feel you have a strong enough relationship with a networking partner to try generating referrals then and there, give it a go!

The best ways to use one-to-one meetings to promote yourself

To finish up this section, there are a couple of key concepts to mention that will help you, the Unnatural Promoter, build a better business.

1. Never stop relationship-building

A quick story. A few years ago, Steve, a BNI member, proudly told his group that he'd had a one-to-one with every single member. He was, in effect, telling them that he had completed his task. About three months later, I was talking to Steve, and he told me that the referrals he was receiving from the group had dropped off.

It didn't take long to work out that the two events were related. Not only had he stopped doing one-to-ones, he had only completed the round of Getting to Know You one-to-ones.

I encouraged him to do a Business Builder one-to-one – and guess what? The relationship he already had with that other member got him a referral to someone who became a key client.

Relationship-building is a journey, not a destination. This means that you are never 'done' with relationship-building: it is an ongoing process. We are trying to get other people to promote us and our business – if we don't stay top of mind by continuing to build on what has gone before, we won't be successful.

So, there is one important question that you need to ask at every single one-to-one meeting – whatever level of relationship you are already at with your partner:

'When's our next one-to-one going to be?'

You are never going to be able to find out everything you need to know about someone in one meeting, and of course, over time, things get forgotten. Times also change – we continue to take on new clients, work on different projects, or work towards new goals. Don't forget, as we saw in Chapter 3, that it takes at least 90 hours to get a relationship to the closeness required to pass good quality referrals to one another.

2. The Givers Give mentality

In Chapter 3, we discussed how you can get referrals faster if you give to others, using the law of reciprocity. This can absolutely apply here when it comes to one-to-one meetings.

A typical one-to-one might last about an hour, so each partner has half an hour on themselves. Obviously, it never quite happens like that – the conversation flows this way and that – but on average, that is how it works.

What about a different approach? Let me tell you about Sam. We'd known each other a bit, and agreed to catch up over a coffee one day. What happened next amazed me.

I was already planning to ask Sam about himself and his business. But before I could get a word in, Sam said he wanted to focus this meeting all on me. Instead of splitting the time between us, he had this hour that he wanted to use to help me. I tried to protest, but he was having none of it.

Over the course of the hour, he generated several opportunities for me – different referrals, people I should connect with – and true to his word, didn't focus on his business once.

Sam was employing what I would term a 'Givers Give' mentality. He was giving without expecting anything in return. Except, of course, it was going to come back to him in return, because of the law of reciprocity. All I could think both during and after our meeting was 'How can I help *you*?' How could I do anything else?

So we arranged a follow-up – where of course the tables were turned, and I focused solely on helping him.

Chapter 7: Action Steps

➤ What networking have you done recently? Has it mostly been at larger networking events? Have you taken the time to build relationships with your network on a one-on-one basis?

➤ Prepare your 4 Key Questions for your next one-to-one meeting. Type up the answers ready to send as soon as you set up the meeting.

➤ Ask your one-to-one partners to send you answers to the 4 Key Questions so you can get to know them before you meet.

➤ Work out who you would like introductions to so you can share them at your one-to-ones, and have stories prepared to demonstrate how good you are.

➤ At every one-to-one, make sure you ask: 'When's our next one-to-one going to be?'

➤ Try having a one-to-one where you don't talk about you. Make it all about helping them.

8 Networking Strategically

In life, there's an old maxim that says 'It's not *what you know*, it's *who you know*'. But it isn't the complete picture when it comes to networking. What's more important is *how well you know them*. In the last chapter, we looked at getting to know people through one-to-ones. However, we need to take it one step further. What we really need to consider is *who they know* to be able to promote ourselves as effectively as possible.

After all, we could build deep relationships with people who just can't help us with the referrals we want. Accepting there is randomness when networking, and we never know who people know, being more strategic with the people we build relationships with might get us a better return. Can we get the right team around us?

That certainly suits me as an Unnatural Promoter because I need to do less promoting.

Putting it all together

A few years ago, Tim Cook, my co-National Director of BNI, and I were asked if we would have time for a meeting. Nothing too strange about that: requests like this come in on a regular basis.

But this was different. Usually when someone asks for a meeting, a business owner pitches to you. Not eight business owners. Let me be clear – this wasn't one company that had sent eight people along to a meeting, it was eight different businesses that were all pitching for business. But they were doing so collectively.

They were led by Andy, who was a branding consultant. Alongside him was a copywriter, a graphic designer, a photographer, a marketing company, a videographer, a PR company and a web agency.

They were all involved in one combined pitch, each playing a greater or lesser role depending on the need for their service. They had even branded themselves (it stands to reason given the types of businesses involved) as Riverside Creatives: they were all members a of a BNI group in Putney, south-west London, that met in a venue alongside the River Thames.

Tim and I were blown away by the way the group presented themselves. They were all small businesses, with between one and nine employees – but they came across like a much bigger business, encompassing departments and different specialisms. They also created a lot of referrals for each other.

Let's have a look at some of the reasons why their approach worked so well.

1. They were related businesses, but not competing

All Riverside Creatives' constituent businesses were in the creative industry, but crucially, they were different. They didn't compete. When one of them took a new client on, the odds were that they would bring in one or more of the others.

As an example, Andy, as the branding specialist, would regularly introduce the web agency after he had designed the look and feel for a client. Then, the client would typically want to upgrade the copy and imagery on their materials, so the copywriter and photographer would be introduced.

Referrals passed around the group constantly – because they were all talking to clients about areas of business that they could all be involved in.

2. They shared the same target market

As all the separate businesses involved were able to refer each other on a regular basis, it stood to reason that if they practised being targeted with their networking (as we saw in Chapter 6), they all benefited.

When one asked specifically for their dream referral, they all could get in with them too – so they all asked for dream referrals. This meant they cast the net much wider in asking for referrals from their respective networks.

3. They created an image of a much bigger business

As I mentioned, Tim and I were surprised when eight business owners came to a meeting. It appeared that we were talking to a much larger business – and the impression was enhanced because they had branded themselves together.

But it also gave them an advantage when asking for referrals. Instead of each of them only being able to ask for referrals into similar level businesses as themselves as individuals, they were able to pitch to (and win work with) much bigger businesses.

4. Their group went from strength to strength

The group consistently attracted potential new members because they were passing so much business. At one point, they lost their web development company due to a geographical move, and it was no longer practical to bring them into pitches and jobs.

So, they cast their net out and almost immediately had five new web agencies keen to be involved. The group then chose the right company who was the best fit and would bring the most value.

They were part of a larger BNI group (with all the other trades and professions), but they found it easy to grow their mini group because of the obvious amount of business being passed among them.

Riverside Creatives were very successful and represent the dream scenario for any business owner to try to replicate when networking.

In BNI, Andy and his colleagues had created what is known as a 'Power Team' – a group of related businesses that work together to create a much larger whole than they ever could individually. That is the term applied once the group is working successfully.

Until then, you have just got to start thinking about building relationships with businesses in related industries.

Which industry grouping are you in?

Related industries to your own are a great starting point. This diagram shows a standard breakdown of typical industry groupings that you might like to build to promote yourself with:

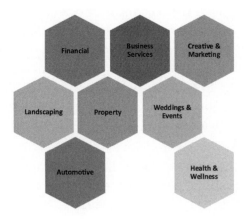

Many business owners will find these groupings help define the businesses they should surround themselves with – it is clear who they have a synergy with. The trades working in the property sector are an obvious example – if a builder takes on a new client, they can bring in an electrician, plumber, carpenter, decorator and so on.

But there are some points to think about when deciding what your industry grouping should be:

➤ A business can sit in more than one industry group. For example, a florist would often be considered to sit with the Events group – for example, for wedding flowers. However, many florists offer a corporate service providing fresh flowers for reception areas. This would sit more naturally with Business Services.

➤ The florist example illustrates that it is your target market that really defines your industry grouping. I know an insurance broker (typically in Financial) who specialises in landlord insurance. He wants referrals to estate and lettings agents, so it makes much more sense for him to align himself with the Property group. The key is to think which of the industry groupings deal with your target market the most.

➤ The industry groupings in the diagram aren't exhaustive. They are generic headings that cover the majority of businesses. Note that there are a couple of other groups in there – for example, automotive or landscaping. I know a number of BNI groups that have professionals from these sectors that work together well. In the automotive group, they include new car sales, used car sales, a car-finding service, bodywork repair, car-servicing and dent removal. Most importantly, they all regularly deal with clients that could be useful to each other.

There are, then, no hard-and-fast rules about industry groupings. It just comes down to what works for a given business and the target market they are going for.

What is important is that the group of businesses look for referrals for each other. You can put a group of related businesses together, but with no organisation or cohesion, they will only ever be a collection of different businesses. Get it working, and you can have a Power Team of businesses all trying to promote you, leading to more business for all.

How many related businesses do you need promoting you?

There is no correct answer to this – other than saying more is better than less. Let's take a moment to look at what difference it makes when you have other businesses around you.

Assuming you haven't yet started building any referral relationships with related businesses, how many people can promote you? Obviously the answer is zero. You have got no one to work with.

So, let's add someone in. With two of you, how many relationships are there between you? Picture each relationship as a handshake: two people shaking hands signifies one relationship.

One is better than none – but it doesn't come anywhere close to a functioning team like the Riverside Creatives group. Let's add a third person then – there are now three relationships that can create referral opportunities for each other.

Now is where it starts to get interesting. Adding a fourth person in creates six relationships, a fifth moves it on to ten. Add a sixth – and there are now 15 relationships working between the participants of the group. Remember, that means that if each individual were to shake hands with every other individual there would be fifteen handshakes.

You can see this summarised in this diagram:

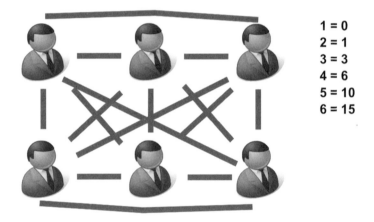

1 = 0
2 = 1
3 = 3
4 = 6
5 = 10
6 = 15

Those of you that are mathematically minded will see a pattern developing here; those of you who aren't probably weren't expecting a maths lesson right now – but there is a mathematical formula to illustrate this.

No. of relationships = $\dfrac{n^2 - n}{2}$

(where 'n' is the number of people in the group)

As the size of the group grows, the relationships that will exist within the group (as indicated by the number of handshakes) will grow exponentially.

A group of eight people will have 28 relationships in play – and that is plenty to maximise the opportunity of referrals being passed within the group.

So, bigger is better – although there will come a point where it gets too large to manage. Ten people would have 45 relationships.

There is a lot of evidence about the ideal size of a group when it comes to productivity. Robert Sutton, a professor of organisational behaviour at Stanford University, studied this and concluded that the most productive meetings have up to eight people in attendance (see Axtell 2018).

When groups of related businesses meet, there will be discussion around the group. If too many people try to have their say, the quality of the conversation will inevitably suffer, meaning the group will be less effective at promoting one another to get referrals.

Turning your businesses into a Power Team

It is one thing having a group of related businesses. It is quite another to turn them into a high-performing Power Team like Riverside Creatives.

The main thing the group needs to do to is to meet regularly. It doesn't really matter where the Power Team meets – it could be at the premises of one of the businesses, in a local restaurant or coffee shop, or online.

Building relationships with each of the other members of the group will be vital – as we saw in Chapter 3, there is no way that referrals can be passed among one another unless each person feels comfortable to do so.

But there's another key reason why meeting regularly is so important. Business moves fast – how often do you take on new clients or start working on new projects? Keeping each other updated is crucial if you want to build a strong and productive Power Team.

Here are some topics that could be discussed when the Power Team meets:

1. **Latest client and project updates**
   Who is everyone working with? Who has taken on a new client that other members might be interested in an introduction to? Have any projects taken on a new direction? There are no competing businesses here: there is opportunity for all given that the businesses share similar target markets.

2. **Specific referral requests**
   Who does everyone want referrals to? Given you are surrounded by related businesses, it should increase the chances of success when being specific. Then, when describing what each business can do for them, further potential referrals are likely to open up for others.

3. **What potential collaborations are there?**
   Using Riverside Creatives' approach, there is an opportunity for Power Team members to pitch together for work. They have the ability then to try and win much larger pieces of work than they would otherwise be able to on their own.

4. **What professions do they need in the Power Team?**
   Assuming the Power Team isn't getting too big and unwieldy, the group could take time to

brainstorm other trades and professions they would like in their number. It would be well worth the group inviting guests in suitable professions along from time to time to witness what the group are doing for each other.

5. **Is there any marketing material the group can work on together?**
Some successful Power Teams brand themselves, and produce marketing collateral. You'll need to think carefully about this, as there may be incoming and outgoing members of the Power Team, but it can present the group very effectively.

A last word on Power Teams

If you're reading this book, it is likely that you are an Unnatural Promoter. That means you probably aren't yet promoting yourself and networking effectively... *yet*.

Please be clear that what's in this chapter is an advanced networking technique. To get to a position where you have a functioning and productive Power Team, all working together to promote each other and generate referrals, takes time. It won't come overnight.

It will typically be as part of a larger organisation: it is very unlikely that you would start forming your own Power Team from scratch tomorrow. The Riverside Creatives group were all members of a BNI group – meaning there was some structure behind what they were doing.

That said, having a group of related businesses to yours around you will make a massive difference to your ability to generate referrals. BNI estimates that two thirds of referrals come from members' related businesses.

So, if you can get the right businesses around you, you'll get more referrals. And that means less promoting yourself – which is great for Unnatural Promoters.

Chapter 8: Action Steps

> ➤ Who is in your network now? Are they related businesses to yours, or are they unconnected? Surrounding yourself with more of the former will help (you don't have to forget the latter though!).

> ➤ List all the professions and business categories that fall in your industry grouping. These will be the businesses that typically pass business to you.

> ➤ Determine which of the groups your business sits in. Then think about various products/services you sell, and whether each one means it would be appropriate to target different groupings.

> ➤ Over time, look to build a Power Team of around eight businesses that work together to find business for each other. Do this by building relationships with them, and then asking if they'd like to formalise the Power Team relationship. This becomes much easier when you join an organisation like BNI, as there is a level of structure and accountability that makes it happen more effectively.

> ➤ When you have a Power Team, meet regularly to discuss current projects, target clients, and how you can work together.

9 Promoting on Social Media

It's time for a quick check on where we're up to. So far, we have looked at several ways to help other people to promote us. The key to all of them has been that if we can build a good relationship with them, and then do certain things (sharing your Why, telling them stories, being clear on our target market), they will be far more inclined to promote us.

But there are also other ways we can promote ourselves. The activities in Chapters 9 and 10 are on us, but as discussed at the very beginning, we're not looking at activities that necessitate vast expense. All of them will help make the phone ring with potential business opportunities.

Why should you promote yourself on social media?

There are plenty of other people and other books far more qualified to talk about the power of social media than I am, but my take on it for Unnatural Promoters is this: in the modern world, if you're not online, then you're missing out.

Clearly in a post Covid-19 world, everyone has had to adapt to online. But the principles behind networking online and face to face are essentially the same. The only difference is the platform – whether you're meeting people online or in the real world.

When online, you can build relationships, you can hear stories about how contacts in your network have helped others, and you can source referrals for both yourself and other people. At the same time, you can be hard sold to, or meet people who are only interested in themselves and what they've got to say.

Here's why social media is such a good way to promote yourself.

1. It is quick and easy

It is easy to connect with people at the click of a button. At the same time, you can network with people from the comfort of your own home, or on the move from your smartphone.

2. You can build a large network

Networking online is a great way to build up the size of your network, whether you use LinkedIn, Facebook, Instagram, Twitter or any other platform. Geography is irrelevant: connections can be down the road or on the other side of the world.

There is one caveat. I've argued throughout that strong relationships are vital – and face-to-face networking will always be better for this. If you're only online, then it's going to be so much harder.

You have got to find a happy balance between networking online (building the breadth of your network) and in person (building the depth of your network).

3. It's easy to find the right place to promote yourself

The internet is a big place, and while it may initially seem daunting, it is relatively easy to make your online promotion much more targeted.

For example, searching under hashtags means that you can instantly be taken to relevant content for you. Posts you make should have relevant hashtags for you – and be explicit about what searches your content will appear in. For example – instead of just using #property, if your specialism is #equityrelease, use that hashtag as well.

In addition, some of the major platforms have group functionality, where you can pick your topic and find discussions all grouped together.

I remember a conversation with an old colleague, Ruth. She wasn't convinced about the value of social media, and thought it was just people posting pictures of what they were having for lunch. While you do get that, I wanted to demonstrate that whatever your interests are, there are communities discussing those topics.

Ruth was into horses, and a quick search on LinkedIn showed us that there were a vast array of groups devoted to equine-related activities. And that was on LinkedIn – a platform generally more business focused than, say, Facebook.

4. It's easy to position yourself as an expert

Once you've found the best places on the internet to promote yourself, it is possible over time to demonstrate your credibility within these areas.

You will build your visibility by posting content, commenting and engaging with other people's posts. Over time, assuming you are adding value through your posts/comments/engagements, you will build your reputation within the areas you focus on. Do this well, and you will find that you will appear in other people's searches – they will potentially now start following you.

Note that even if you don't feel confident writing your own posts, even sharing other people's posts (providing they are relevant) can help increase your credibility as an expert in your field.

Which online platforms should I be on?

There are a multitude of different social network platforms – and from the time of writing to the point when you read this, another load will have sprung up. As such, I'm not going to cover them all. Please note that what I share here comes simply from my experience promoting myself with each of the different networks. Each social network offers something slightly different – although there is a lot of crossover between them.

Facebook

It took me some years to warm up to using Facebook – for a long time I was one of those 'lurkers' using my other half's profile to snoop around. I was spending so much time doing that I thought I really should get my own!

Facebook is probably the most social of the networks. From seeing what friends and colleagues are up to, to chatting with them, the time I spend on Facebook is mostly downtime – the sort of thing you'll do at the end of the day to relax and unwind.

A scan through my recent Facebook posts reveals a lot of family posts, BNI posts (but that feels like family given the nature of the organisation), and posts about my football team (Spurs, in case you're wondering). This stands to reason, as it is all about building relationships.

What I don't do is promote myself. Of course, there are plenty of people who do promote themselves and their business – and Facebook itself generates huge income from advertising revenue – but for an Unnatural Promoter I would argue it's not the best place to start.

Instagram

Instagram was the social network I started using most recently – and to be honest, I am still learning about it. It is much like Facebook in that it is very much a social network – I certainly only really use it in downtime. The key here is that every post has either a picture or a video, which immediately makes the posts much more engaging than if they were just text.

Instagram is growing fast, and at the time of writing has three-and-a-half times the monthly users that Twitter has. The big appeal is to the younger demographic – according to Statista.com (2016, 2021) , 69 per cent of Instagram users are younger than 35 years old (see also Ahlgren 2021).

Businesses also use Instagram to promote themselves, especially if pictures promote what they do. For instance,

98 per cent of fashion brands use Instagram. Should you use it to promote yourself? If visual images of what you do are important, then you should consider it.

Twitter

Twitter was my first port of call on my own social media journey, in large part because I loved the fact you could only write posts of 140 characters. (Twitter now allows 280 characters, but Twitter says that even now only 12 per cent of tweets use more than 140.) Writing long replies to messages always felt like a chore, so 140 characters was brilliant because I could be brief!

This brevity does help the Unnatural Promoter. You can help position yourself as an expert in your field just by sharing links to good quality, relevant content about your industry. You can easily add a comment to other people's tweets, which can further demonstrate your credibility in your field, and it also creates engagement.

As ever in networking, engagement and relationships are key. Being realistic, there is only so much engagement possible due to the small posts – but you can still build a relationship on Twitter.

LinkedIn

I've left LinkedIn to last because I believe it is the one that anyone reading this book should absolutely be using. I would certainly say that I'm still on my LinkedIn journey – I've only started using it 'properly' in the last couple of years, despite having an account for a long time.

It is the most relevant social network because of the demographics of its users. Whereas the other platforms started off for social purposes but now have businesses using them, LinkedIn is unashamedly business focused. The CEO of LinkedIn, Jeff Weiner, has said he wants LinkedIn to be the home of all working professionals across the world. To help illustrate this point, 91 per cent of business marketers say that LinkedIn is the top place to find quality content (compared to 29 per cent for Twitter and 27 per cent for Facebook).

There is also the potential to receive referrals from LinkedIn. While there are never any guarantees, if the whole point of networking is to grow your business through receiving referrals, then LinkedIn needs to be considered. According to LinkedIn, 80 per cent of business-to-business social media leads originate from within the network.

There is no doubt that I've made more self-promoting posts on LinkedIn than on any other network. Why? I think because LinkedIn is focused on business – maybe subconsciously I've been less keen to promote myself elsewhere because I think non-business contacts will be judging more.

(For data on LinkedIn, see 99firms 2021; Gallant 2021; LinkedIn 2017; Wohlsen 2014.)

What should I post about?

Don't worry! I recognise that us Unnatural Promoters are on a journey to feeling comfortable about posting content on social media. My old fears rear up: will people like what I've got to say (and literally so in terms of counting the number of 'likes'), or will they challenge me because they don't agree with me?

Give it a go, though. According to Foundation Inc., of the worldwide 250 million monthly LinkedIn users, only three million post content on a weekly basis. That might sound like a lot, but it's only one per cent. If you are prepared to be brave and put even the odd piece of content up, you will automatically be more visible than the majority: three million users are getting nine billion impressions every week.

There are three different types of posts that will help you promote yourself:

1. Educational posts

These are where you demonstrate your knowledge of your sector/industry. They might be articles you read in the news shared with a quick comment or your opinion attached, or your view on the latest trends. If posting your opinions still makes you worry, remember you are an expert in what you do, and it is okay for people to disagree with you.

To build credibility even faster, writing your own material in the form of a blog works very well as you're then providing content for other people to share. Put simply, a blog is an article that is posted online. You can create a dedicated blogging site or include a content section on your own website. If you don't want to have to pull that together, you can post articles on LinkedIn. Wherever you do it though, if you can create a consistent flow of content, and then share it widely via the networks listed above, you'll start building a following that wants to hear what you've got to say.

Articles don't need to be long – people lose attention if the article goes on and on. Approximately 500-1000 words is perfect, or as Heather Townsend (2014), author of *The Financial Times Guide to Business Networking* says, about the time it takes to have a cuppa.

Blog content should be related to your industry, and specifically demonstrating your expertise or point of view.

2. Sharing successes

This is where you highlight that you've been taken on by a new client, or talking about a win that you've created for one of your clients. To help with the awkward feeling of not wanting to boast, express it from the point of view of the client – for example, you might ask your client what value they've had from your service, then post what **they** tell you **they've** had from you. Even better, if they post about how pleased they were with your service, make sure you re-share their post.

The more you can demonstrate social proof of what others think about you, the better the results of what the post might bring (as well as it being more likely you'll put the post up in the first place). You may of course have to remove names from the post if it wouldn't be appropriate to share them – just refer to them as 'a client' – but if you can refer to them by name or company name, all the better.

3. What you are doing on a given day

I'm not talking here about 'what I had for lunch' posts (seriously, up to you on those, but they're just not for me), but there is value to be gained by people knowing what you're doing.

Remember that social media is just a platform for you to network with other people. The main aim of networking is to build relationships, and when you have a relationship with someone, they will be interested in what you're doing or where you're going. It's really important to demonstrate that you are a real human being – it's much easier to build a relationship and empathise with someone whom you can see is going through similar life events or challenges to yourself.

Having gone through the various social networks, it's clear that you will be posting different content to each one, but relationships are strengthened by knowing what you are doing, especially when it includes your family, your friends, your clients or your work colleagues. When they are tagged, their networks will also see your post, which will, over time, increase your visibility and credibility further.

Using video to promote yourself

It only takes a second or two of scrolling through a social media feed or viewing a website or two to realise how important video is. It is everywhere, and in a world where everyone has a smartphone and can create video content at the push of a button, it is impossible to ignore.

When you see a video or a block of text on your Facebook feed, which grabs you more? Compared to a picture, there's so much more that can be put into a video. Video is simply more dynamic – it grabs people's attention.

A video that is well put together, with a good message, can be a compelling way to help you position yourself as an expert in your field.

However, there's an elephant in the room to deal with first...

You're never going to get me on camera!

For us Unnatural Promoters, it's one thing to get us to shout about ourselves at all – but on video, where there's a permanent record of it, and where every flaw is there for everyone to see – no way!

I actually don't mind the filming. Admittedly, I've done a lot of it now, so I'm sure that practice, as in most parts of life, has made it a lot easier. My issue is when I'm about to press send on the post with my video in.

There are a couple of reasons why many people don't like to be filmed. The first one is that people think that they look strange when they see themselves on video.

The problem is that the way we see our own face differs from how everyone else does. We only ever see ourselves in the mirror, which, by its very nature, shows us a mirror image of what we actually look like. Since our faces aren't symmetrical, that mirror image is slightly different to the reality – and the version we see when we're filmed.

Look at these two versions of my profile picture. The one on the left is how the world sees me – the one on the right is how I see myself:

This phenomenon was studied (see Ayres 2017) by researchers at the University of Wisconsin-Milwaukee in the 1970s. Participants were asked to look at real and mirror images of their own faces, and those of their friends and family (without being told that that was what they were looking at).

The results were clear: people preferred their own mirror images but preferred the real versions of others. Participants also couldn't describe *why* they picked one image over the other – the differences were too subtle.

It's these differences that make many people uncomfortable with being on video. They are barely noticeable to your consciousness, but your brain knows the difference, and prefers the mirrored you, because that's what it is used to.

It's a similar problem when we hear our own voice. Being recorded on a video will mean that we hear how we speak like everyone else does – i.e. the sound waves will hit our ear drums. However, we hear our own voice inside our head differently. When we speak (and of course, there's a more scientific way of putting this), the sound goes from our vocal chords, into our skull, and then to our ears. When it travels through the bone of your skull, it is distorted. Our interpretation of our voice is different to what everyone else hears.

So, Unnatural Promoters – if we're going to get around these issues, we have to tell ourselves that what we're seeing and hearing isn't what everyone else is seeing and hearing: it's our brains playing tricks with us. I promise you – no one else will think anything other than it's 100 per cent you!

The second issue many worry about when being filmed is confirmation bias. This is the tendency people have to pay more attention to things that back up what we believe is true.

This means that if we believe we look strange on camera, or if we think that we're not a natural (and usually, the people we see on screens are highly paid actors and professionals), then we will watch the footage looking for examples to confirm our beliefs. When we see them – as inevitably we will because we're not television professionals – we dwell on them.

How often do we focus on one piece of negative feedback because it outweighs in our mind the ten pieces of positivity received? When I've done a training session or a talk for a group of, say, 100 people, there will be 99 excellent or good responses, and one 'room for improvement'. Which one do you think I dwell on?

Promoting myself on camera

For BNI UK/Ireland, I am the public face of the business. Once I'd made my peace with it, I had to start working out how I would promote myself in that role.

In a membership organisation, I realised that it was important for the leadership to not be 'in the ivory tower', but to be visible and obvious to BNI's customers. One way to achieve this would be to visit the groups – but a more effective way was using video.

I have made and distributed videos on a regular basis. Some are educational, some are fun, some are recognition based – but each one, either shared directly with a group, or more widely distributed on social media, has made me more well known within the organisation.

I regularly meet people and they swear blind that they've met me before. I know for a fact we haven't met – they're remembering me from video. I'm far more visible within the BNI network than if I'd tried to meet every member in person.

So how did I, an Unnatural Promoter, manage to do this? And not only that, but appeared to be natural at it?

I think that the key here was to consciously tell myself that I wasn't promoting myself. I know it was me on camera, but the reason I was doing it wasn't for myself. As I was doing it for the business, it made it okay.

If I'm now doing video as a promotion for myself, I apply a similar approach. Instead of it being about me, I try to think about how the intended audience would view it. My target audience are people who lack confidence to network and promote themselves: when I go on camera, I'm doing it for them, rather than doing it for me.

More recently, I've started doing more videos via Facebook Live. This is where you can 'go live' within Facebook (LinkedIn also offers this service), and anyone who happens to be online at that moment can watch and interact with you live. (The video is also then saved to your timeline and can be viewed like any other video.)

As you'd expect, the first time I tried these out, it was a scary experience – but over time I've got more practised at doing them. The best way I've found about making them not about me is to use them to have a conversation with someone else.

It makes it feel to me like the other person is the one being promoted, although I'm getting the same benefits as well. You can either sit together behind the camera, or there is software you can use that will put you both on the screen. I use one called BeLive (https://belive.tv) – it works really well.

How to make videos that promote you better

Just to be clear, I'm not an expert in videography – seek professional advice! A lot of my learnings have come from the excellent Dave Foulkes and Ed Lawrence at **https://businessfilmbooth.com** (check them out, especially if you're in the Hertfordshire area – they're awesome).

That said, as the story above illustrates, I've now made a lot of videos, so I've been able to pick up a few tips to share with you. As ever, they come from the angle of encouraging Unnatural Promoters to give it a try.

➤ **Use your phone camera.** No budget to use professionals? Not a problem. The cameras in smartphones are so good that they'll produce easily high enough quality video for our purposes. It is better to use the camera on the back of the phone, rather than the front, 'selfie' camera, as they tend to be better quality.

➤ **Use landscape mode.** The shape of your social media feed is landscape, so if you film portrait, you're only ever going to get a smaller vertical image with blanked out sections either side.

➤ **Shorter is better.** Our attention span isn't long – between 30 and 60 seconds is about right. People just won't watch videos that last several minutes.

➤ **Look into the lens.** And I mean stare at it! It feels unnerving at first, but it's vital, because then the viewer feels you're looking at them. Imagine talking to someone and they were constantly looking over your shoulder – how would that feel? It is the same if you don't look at the lens directly. The viewer feels that you're not looking at them directly, distracting them from what you're saying.

➤ **Remember your lines.** One of the reasons why the videos I've done with Filmbooth are so good is that they are chunked down. I don't ever have to remember too much in one go. Not so easy when using your smartphone, so learning what you're going to say is important – further backing up why it is better if it is shorter. If I need to remember a number, a name or a date, I'll write them large in marker pen, keeping the paper as close to the lens as possible, so my eyes stay close to the lens.

➤ **Make sure you're well lit.** You don't need to invest in studio-quality lighting, but just making sure that any natural light is on your face (rather than having a window behind you) will make a big difference. To provide a little extra light on your face, you can buy a clip-on light for less than a fiver.

➤ **You need to be heard.** Clearly sound is important when creating video, so ensure you are in a quiet place. If you're shooting outside or in a busy location, you will need a microphone.

➤ **Avoid double chins!** Okay, I can't promise that entirely, but videos (and photos) are much more flattering if the camera is just above the subject – i.e. looking up slightly at the camera.

➤ **Hold it steady.** There's not much that's worse when viewing a video if the camera is shaky – it distracts completely from your message. If you've got a tripod, great, or resting the camera on a hard surface works too. That's much better than trying to do a selfie video, and then your arm starts to ache...

➤ **Get someone to help you.** Apart from the fact that a friend can do the actual filming, I've found that having someone else there makes it more real – I'm not just talking to the camera anymore. They can also be useful to talk over wording.

➤ **Get subtitles.** You video will be viewed on phones more than anywhere else. It isn't always possible to have the sound up, so having subtitles in your videos is important (as well as making them accessible to deaf people). A simple solution is www.rev.com, where they create captions for a nominal fee per minute of content.

➤ **Practise, practise, practise.** Oh, and then practise some more. It feels strange at first, but then you get better. I do get people telling me they'll never look like I do on camera: but trust me, it looks natural because I've done hundreds of videos. And if I've done that many videos, think how many takes I've done...

The key to social media

The clue to social media is in its name. It is *social*. It means engagement with people and having conversations. That's why I believe that online networking is the same as in-person networking – just in a different setting.

If it is not social, it is just broadcasting. In a face-to-face world, broadcasting is like going to a networking event and only ever having one-way conversations. People might listen initially, but the effect will soon wear off.

It's much better to approach promoting yourself on social media as primarily a way of building relationships. Do this, and you'll get people wanting to shout about you and promote you.

One last thing: and this happens regularly among small business owners. Having been reminded that social media is important, it's easy to get into a cycle where you are active, and then less so. You'll then get another reminder, and it starts again.

Promoting yourself effectively on social media means having a consistent approach, not peaks and troughs. If you can't manage multiple social media channels, don't! Pick the one or two that work for your business and life and stick to them. It doesn't look great for credibility when you find dormant social media accounts, with a last post from back in 2014!

Chapter 9: Action Steps

➤ Work out what the best social network is for you and your business. Is it LinkedIn, Facebook, Instagram, Twitter – or something else?

➤ If you haven't already got an account set up – do so.

➤ Think about what you can post. Remember that consistency is key, so plan an hour in your diary per month to schedule your posts. Don't aim for too much! If you can do one post per month, that's better than nothing.

➤ Research what people in your industry are posting. Can you like/comment/share? Connect with people who are sharing content relevant to you and your business. Use the hashtags that they're using.

➤ Try writing a blog. In time you may want to set up a dedicated blog section on your website, but this needs consistent content. To get started, post your blog as an article on LinkedIn.

➤ Record your first video. Pick a topic related to your business that interests you, and film a short (approximately one-minute) video about that topic. Post it on your preferred network – and see what happens!

➤ Be social! When someone reaches out to you to connect, talk to them, find out about them, build a relationship.

Case Study 3
Bryony Thomas

It started with a Facebook post. Bryony Thomas was asking for help.

Bryony Thomas
✓ Moderator · 8 October 2018

Who can help me with this?

Following yet another conference at which I struggled to chat to people I didn't already know, and regularly flustered the 'what do you do' question... I've decided to make this my development area for a little while.

Who could help me craft some sensible and compelling ways of answering typical networking questions? And, is anyone here good at working with introverts, who end up coming across as cold?

 Julie Holmes, Lynda Shaw and 11 others   33 comments

As you might imagine, given my tendencies as a fellow introverted Unnatural Networker, her post was speaking to me. What got me about the post, though, was that it came from someone I wouldn't have expected it to come from.

I didn't know Bryony well at all at the time. We were connected through being members of the Professional Speaking Association (the post itself was in a PSA Members group) – but all I really knew of her was that she was a successful business owner and top-level professional speaker.

How on earth was someone who I perceived to be at such a high level of credibility struggling to promote herself while out networking?

When we chatted, Bryony talked about an amusing scene in the film *Notting Hill*. In the scene, Will Thacker, the lead character played by Hugh Grant, takes his new girlfriend Anna Scott (Julia Roberts) round to dinner at a friend's house. The amusement comes because one of his friends has no idea that Anna is a famous Hollywood movie star.

'I mean, last film you did, what did you get paid?' he asks, expecting a low figure and trying to make the point that it is a hard life scraping together a living as an actor. A mumbled 'Fifteen million dollars' response comes back.

Clearly the aim was to get a laugh from the viewer, but there's an interesting point in that instead of just being open that she's a major movie star, Anna downplays herself, and everyone feels embarrassed by the situation.

Bryony mentioned this not to compare herself to a famous movie star, but to illustrate how she approaches people asking her the 'What do you do?' question. For example, at the school gates, another parent might ask her what she does, and instead of promoting herself honestly and telling them that she is one of the UK's foremost marketing thinkers and runs a successful national marketing business based on her bestselling book, the response from Bryony will typically come back with something like 'I do a bit of marketing'.

The conversation might then hint at what she does, or the other person might try to be nice and offer help in some way ('Would you like to be introduced to the graphic designer I know?') – but the reality is the conversation doesn't help Bryony or the other person at all.

In fact, as in the scene from *Notting Hill*, they both tend to go away from it feeling embarrassed, because Bryony didn't promote herself effectively. It's not that she's not good at what she does: she simply isn't very good at *saying* she's good at what she does.

So where do Bryony's challenges come from?

What's interesting is that when you delve into her past, it sounds like Bryony isn't an Unnatural Promoter at all. She's always been happy to put herself out there – for example, when she was a teenager, she organised litter picks and invited the local newspaper along to cover it. She was able to do this because she wasn't doing it for herself, to be popular – it was about doing something good in the world. As a student, she got into student politics, and was active as a campaigner. Her rationale for doing this is the same: as a campaigner, you aren't really promoting yourself – it's more about championing a wider cause. For Bryony this is about 'showing up, not showing off'.

Sticking with the political theme at university, she then found herself running for student union president. This was much more personal, as it most definitely was about her – and unfortunately, she didn't win. However, this was partly down to the campaign going south when her campaign messages were sabotaged, and images of her were doctored. Based on this treatment, it's a wonder she's prepared to put herself out there at all.

But perhaps the biggest indicator of her self-promotion challenges has to date back to what she remembers of her father when growing up. Her overriding memory of what her dad used to say to her were phrases like 'Keep your feet on the ground, my love', or 'There's a long way to fall from up there'. Her dad was coming from a protective, fatherly place – but it had the effect of making her believe that she shouldn't be climbing too high or shining too brightly.

This built up and ingrained her inner voice and meant that over time, while being extremely driven and ambitious, she was uncomfortable in talking about her achievements.

So how has Bryony managed to build a successful business?

The first link I made when hearing her story, and particularly the part about her dad, was that it was now clear why she chose a career in marketing. You might think that marketing would be the last profession an Unnatural Promoter would pick, because you have to promote: but the emotional connection is clear here.

As well as her dad's view that staying small and unseen was a route to staying safe, she was also brought up among nonconformist adults who went on marches and confronted injustice. There's a warrior or campaigning side to what Bryony does. She goes into battle for a cause. She mainly works on promoting other people and their causes, which is much easier for her to do. This balances out in Bryony's mind in the phrase above, 'This is about showing up, not showing off.'

Then – driven by her anti-establishment upbringing – and because she's promoting other people, she's found that her best advice comes when she challenges the norm. Throughout her working life so far, she makes a habit of asking the unaskable question – and if something is unfair, untrue or nonsense, she'll call it. Controversial opinions have helped her to stand out. I definitely need to take a few lessons from her there...

Bryony also gave me some great advice on how she comes across so credibly as a marketing expert and professional speaker. She wrote her excellent book *Watertight Marketing* (2020) so that she can speak about her book, not herself. When presenting on stage, she talks about her clients, not herself.

But perhaps the biggest lesson I took from her was about how most people go about promoting themselves and their business. In her words: 'You don't switch the lighthouse off because no ships have crashed.'

Most people treat promoting themselves as an on/off thing. You do it for a while, then you just get on with running your business. But the problem is, when you need to promote yourself again, it's hard work cranking up the promotional machine, especially if it feels unnatural.

So, while the reticence to 'blow her own trumpet' that led to that Facebook post still exists, Bryony's solution is to think of promoting her business like eating food. She has to eat every day to survive – and she has to promote her business every day for it to survive too. Promoting herself little and often, and with the focus squarely on the book and her clients rather than herself, it becomes more comfortable and habitual, which means it gets done.

10 Promoting by Public Speaking

Heights, spiders, flying, death. Look through any list of the human race's worst fears, and these will commonly appear. Along with one other – public speaking (see Fritscher 2020).

But there's no avoiding it: to promote yourself effectively, public speaking will play a part. This book has focused on how networking will help you promote yourself. Put simply, when you go networking, you will have to speak in public.

Think about a time when you've seen a good speaker. It could have been live, or perhaps a good TED talk. What sort of impression did they create? Were you interested in their product or their cause? Did they position themselves as an expert in their field?

Done well, speaking offers a massive opportunity to promote yourself, and gives your business credibility. The fact that someone has asked you to speak to an audience demonstrates that you have something interesting to say – and means that people will want to listen.

You may not be giving a keynote presentation in front of hundreds of people or delivering a TED talk – but even doing a simple business pitch at a networking group will have the same effect if done well.

There are speakers who command fees for whatever talk they do, and there are plenty of others who use speaking to generate business. If they deliver good value from the stage, members of the audience will engage their consultancy services, or use them as suppliers. As a speaker myself, I have done various 'showcase' talks for no fee that have led on to paid speaking.

There's another very practical reason why speaking in public will help you grow your business. While there is no doubt that it can take a leap of faith to speak to an audience, what do you have to do when you are pitching to a potential client? That may only be a one-on-one 'speech', but the confidence you gain from delivering your message in a broader context will make it easier to do.

In BNI, you lose count of the number of people that you see go through a positive learning journey when it comes to speaking.

The best example of this I ever saw was a young entrepreneur called Mark. I remember visiting his BNI group when he had recently joined – and he was the typical nervous presenter when he spoke. He mumbled his way through a presentation on his carpet-cleaning business, shaking like a leaf, and while the presentation was only 60 seconds long, it felt like an age.

Everyone in the room was just willing him to get through it – although I'm sure there were some just pleased it wasn't them.

About four months later, I attended an end-of-year awards ceremony, and one of the features of the evening was for peer-voted businesses to do a presentation to the room of 400 or so people. They'd been voted on the strength of their presentations to their groups – so you can imagine my surprise when Mark took to the stage.

It was only when he was halfway through that I twigged who it was. But the guy who'd been in such a nervous state just months previously had no notes, engaged with his audience, and delivered a very strong message.

This journey of personal development is important, because if you don't look confident while speaking in public (e.g. when out networking), people may well assume that's what you'd be like in front of a client (if you were referred).

Where can I speak?

There's no substitute for practice when it comes to getting better at public speaking. Of course, you can practise in front of the mirror, or by delivering to a friend or loved one, but to really improve, it takes getting out in front of real people. You'll learn so much more from their reactions and feedback to what you say and how you deliver it.

There are a couple of options of places that you can go to develop your skills.

➤ **Professional Speaking Association (PSA)/ Toastmasters International**
These are specific organisations for people that want to get better at public speaking. The PSA's mission is to help people 'Speak more, speak

better', and is primarily focused on helping speakers build a business from their speaking (whether in direct speaker fees or through using speaking to generate business).

Toastmasters International focuses on helping you improve your communication and build leadership skills. Their focus is less on building a business around speaking, and more on writing speeches and delivering them.

➤ **Networking groups like BNI**
While the primary purpose of networking groups isn't about improving public speaking, there is no question that members see massive personal development, particularly in how to speak in public.

The point with networking groups is they are regular. Whether weekly like BNI, or monthly – the discipline of having to present yourself and your business every time just means you're going to get better at it – even if that might feel a long way away right now.

How to speak better

There are entire books written about public speaking, so there's no way I can do justice to the topic of how to speak in public here – but I can give a few pointers that will help Unnatural Promoters get going with speaking. If you would like to read more, one book I would particularly recommend is *Speak: So Your Audience Will Listen* by Robin Kermode (2013) – full of practical advice that is easy to use straight away.

Let's break down public speaking into four key areas: dealing with nerves, connecting with the audience, using visual aids, and what to say.

Dealing with nerves

Everyone gets nervous when speaking in public. It doesn't matter if it's your first time, or you're a professional speaker who speaks to audiences every day – nerves are completely normal. I speak regularly to audiences of all sizes, and I worry if I'm *not* feeling at least a little bit apprehensive. The heightened adrenalin coursing around my body helps make sure my performance is as good as it can be.

The key is to control signs of nerves. Here's a few things to consider that will help.

1. Practise

Think about how you feel when you have something important to do. Do you like to go into it blind, and wing it? Of course not. You prepare, you practise, you make sure you're as ready as you can be. You can practise on your own, to a friend, or at organisations like the PSA/Toastmasters.

If you haven't got someone to practise with, a mirror can be helpful, or if you can cope with it, video yourself. You will immediately pick up on traits you don't like (for example, saying 'um', or how you're standing) and you can work to try to eradicate them.

2. Using notes

If you can deliver your talk from memory, and do it well, it will heighten your credibility. However, for most people starting out (as well as many who speak regularly) using notes as a memory jogger is fine.

But don't read your presentation out word for word – that would require you to look down too much and not connect with the audience. While you obviously don't want to forget anything – your audience doesn't know what you're going to say, so if you do miss something out, they'll be none the wiser.

Writing your key bullet points on a sheet of paper (provided it is on a table so it doesn't flap around if your hands shake a bit) or cue cards both work well. If prepared, you'll easily be able to say what you need to say on each point – and then, when you need a reminder of what's coming next, grab a quick glance to see the next bullet point.

3. Knowing the set-up

Wherever possible, find out what the layout of the room will be. Where will you be standing? Where will the audience be? Where will you walk onto the stage/enter the space? Where can you put your notes? If showing slides, where's the projector? Where will the computer be? Will you be in the way of projector beam, casting a shadow? Where will you put your water?

The more you can find out, the more prepared you will be. Whenever I've got a big talk to do, I like to physically stand in the space and imagine what it will be like with everyone there.

If that's not possible, make sure you're there early, and watch the speaker(s) before – see where they stand and how they use the space.

Even if you're just presenting your business to a networking group, it's worth thinking about some of the above. How will you best stand to project to the whole room? Do people use the projector? What do other attendees do with their notes?

4. Breathing

When we're about to do a talk, the nervous energy we feel is as a result of the very natural human trait of fight or flight. Fighting or running away won't be the best idea, so we have to find other ways to control our bodies.

Breathing makes a massive difference. I learned this from my friend Andy Bounds – a very successful public speaker. He taught me about 1-4-2 breathing, where, in ratio, you breathe in for 1 second, hold it for 4 seconds, then breathe out for 2 seconds. I double that and go for 2-8-4, repeating it ten times.

This practice of slowing your breathing down and holding the air in your lungs allows more oxygen to enter your bloodstream. You'll feel calmer straight away. I make a habit of doing this just before being introduced to speak – and you can do it in front of other people without them even knowing you're doing it.

Connecting with the audience

One thing that I notice when listening to a top-level professional speaker is that it often appears as if they aren't presenting to the audience so much as having a chat with them. Each individual listening feels as though the speaker is speaking to them personally.

While this is a skill that requires a lot of experience to master, the key thing Unnatural Promoters must do if they want people to buy in to them is connect well with their audience. Here's a few ways you can do this.

1. Smile

It's such a simple point that you might wonder why it even needs to be mentioned. But people are more likely to like you if you radiate warmth and don't look miserable – and a smile is an easy way to do this.

I don't mean you should be grinning like a Cheshire cat throughout your presentation, or after each pause in what you're saying you should look up and fix a grin on your face. But you want to be friendly.

So, as you walk up to start your talk, a genuine smile while looking at the audience will make them warm to you.

2. Body language

Smiling is just one of the non-verbal cues we all give when speaking. How you position yourself, the way you gesture and the way you move all form a part of the message you're trying to get across. If you are uncomfortable, it will be obvious.

I like to plant my feet firmly on the ground, about shoulder width apart, to centre myself. I don't worry about what I'm doing with my hands. Instead I do what I would in a normal conversation with a friend or colleague.

Chances are, when you are trying to get your point across, you use your hands and arms to gesture to help make your point. It's the same when presenting. You will appear less obviously nervous and more 'normal' if you do allow your body to help you express yourself.

What about moving? Everyone is different, and there are some very powerful speakers who stay rooted to the spot, and others who are seemingly constantly on the move. I believe that some movement will add dynamism to your presentation – but the key is to always move with purpose. Don't meander around as this betrays signs of nerves.

The good news is that in many of the scenarios that you, the Unnatural Promoter, will be speaking in – like at networking groups – you'll stand up where you're seated in the room and deliver from there. So keep your feet planted, use your hands – and now we can start to think about looking at the audience.

3. Eye contact

When you're in a one-to-one conversation and the other person doesn't look you in the eye, how does it feel? Obviously it doesn't feel genuine, or perhaps you might think they're trying to hide something.

It's the same when speaking to an audience. Try to make eye contact with as many people as possible by roving your eyes around the room and looking at them. Clearly, you're only going to briefly look at each individual person (staring at one or two isn't a good idea...), but even that moment of eye contact will make them feel like you're speaking to *them*.

As the number in the audience grows, it will become harder if not impossible to catch everyone's eye – but even then, I focus my gaze around as many parts of the room as possible. Start with the back, just running your eyes slowly along the rows – this will make it look like you are getting eye contact even if you can't realistically do so.

4. Using your voice

Your voice will play a big part in how you connect with your audience. No one wants to listen to someone who speaks in a monotone – it gets boring quickly.

You can vary your voice in one of two main ways – volume and speed. You might think that changing volume means speaking normally, and then from time to time raising your voice. But it's easy to get too 'shouty' if you're not careful. Being audible is obviously important, but don't underestimate the power of *lowering* the volume when you're making an important point.

With speed, my general rule is to slow down. I often find that because I'm enthusiastic about what I'm saying, it's very easy to talk far too fast.

Speaking speed is measured in words per minute (wpm). Typical conversation speed is generally somewhere around 120–150 wpm – when giving a speech, this drops slightly to 100–130 wpm (Barnard 2018).

But the key is to vary it. For example, when you're telling a story, you might speed up because the audience is easily following the narrative of the story and they just want to hear what happened. When done, slow down your speech as you reinforce the learnings from the story.

Indeed, at times *silence* can really help you connect with your audience. Allowing a second or two break gives time to process what you're saying and your message.

5. Energy and certainty

Remember, you're trying to promote yourself, and to do that you need to get people to buy in to you. If this is going to happen, they need to believe in you, and one of the best ways to make this happen is to project energy and certainty.

Energy doesn't mean constant movement – it just means radiating positive energy. I often get told after I've done a talk that I come across as very energetic – and that's because I am very enthusiastic about my topic. The enthusiasm and energy show through my movement, my voice, my smile, and the way it feels that I'm just having a chat with the people in the audience.

Certainty is all about you delivering a believable message. You're clear about your thoughts and beliefs. You know what you want to achieve. You're positive about the outcomes you present.

If you're speaking about something that you're passionate about (and let's face it, you should be, given you're talking about your business and your Why) – that energy and certainty will come through loud and clear.

Using visual aids

Including some visuals in your presentation will generally help your audience take in your message better. Humans take in information in one of three ways – auditory, visually and kinaesthetically. Some people will primarily take in your message by *hearing* it, some people prefer to *see* it, while others like to *experience* it – although typically people mix and match.

Approximately two thirds of the world's population are visual learners (whether that's their primary or secondary way of taking in information). If you just speak at them (i.e. in an auditory fashion), they won't take in your message as well as if there are visuals to go alongside the words. Putting a PowerPoint or Keynote presentation together can add a huge amount to the impact of your talk.

It doesn't mean this is necessary for every talk: if you're just delivering a one- or two-minute message, it wouldn't be worth having slides. But for many presentations, slides make a difference. Here's a few pointers to help you put your slides together:

1. Limit the number of words on a slide

The point of using a visual aid is that it supports your presentation: not that the slides **are** your presentation. Unfortunately you will see plenty of presenters that put huge bullet pointed lists of their talk on their slides.

Even worse, they'll read the slides out to the audience. Don't insult your audience's intelligence – they can read the slides themselves; they don't need you to do it for them!

Instead, aim to have just a handful of words on a slide. I genuinely can't remember where I got this advice from, but my aim is to have a maximum of seven words per slide. That's right, just seven!

This can be tough, and I'm not saying that I never create a slide with more – but it's what I'll aim for. The words you then say are either memorised, or you can jot brief notes down on a piece of paper or cue cards (or in the 'notes' section of PowerPoint).

Limiting the number of words you use means the slide will become more shareable. With smartphones, it is easy to snap a quick picture of a slide and share it – so a catchy message along with a hashtag and social media handle will mean your message will be promoted far more widely than to the audience in the room.

2. Use pictures

The phrase 'a picture speaks a thousand words' sums up visual learners, so make sure you include pictures in your slides. They are more interesting to look at than words and will help your audience more easily recall what you said because they'll associate what they heard with images from the slides. If they want the detail, then they'll note it down or you can give them a handout at the end (this must be at the end, otherwise they'll spend the entirety of your presentation reading the handout).

Let's use an example to show you what I mean – see over the page.

How much more visually interesting is the slide underneath compared to the one above? Don't forget that the words spoken for the lower version will be exactly the same as the upper one – it's only the visual that is up for discussion here.

Our Goals

- To hit turnover of £5 million
- To be the number one in our marketplace
- To have a 90% customer satisfaction rate
- To have a happy, motivated workforce
- To see Spurs win the Premier League
- To increase our efficiency by 35%
- To reduce our carbon emissions to net zero by 2030

3. Think about fonts

Make your slides visually appealing. WRITING THE WORDS IN CAPITALS MAKES IT SHOUTY AND MORE DIFFICULT TO READ, while using a basic font like Times New Roman makes it very boring. **Comic Sans might make it look different, but it isn't professional.**

Beware though, if you download and use different fonts, if your presentation is shown from another computer that doesn't have those fonts downloaded, it will revert to a basic font and the formatting will go wrong. It is always worth having a quick run through your slides in the room before you speak to make sure everything looks correct.

Font size is another consideration – especially given there will only be a few words on a slide. The easier it is to read, the better. Even with a sophisticated AV set up including multiple screens, you wouldn't want to use less than a 28-point font size as an absolute minimum.

4. Use slide builds – but don't go mad with animations!

When doing a talk, it is vital that the audience is listening to what you are saying in the moment. If there is other information on the screen at the same time, it is very easy for the mind to wander, read that information and not take it in in the way intended.

Using slide builds gets around this – each different point on a slide appears with a separate click (or you can animate the points to appear after a certain time interval).

However, if you sit and play with PowerPoint, you can come up with all sorts of different ways for your points and pictures to appear on the screen. Cut them out! Unless these builds add to the message, the only one you need is 'Appear'.

What to say

Now let's look at how to put your content together.

1. Make your talk relevant: start with the end in mind

Here I must recommend another book – *The Jelly Effect* by Andy Bounds (2010). He covers this point way better than I ever could, so I'll just highlight a couple of his key points.

He talks about focusing on the 'afters' before anything else – what do you want your audience to do/buy/take action on once you've completed your talk. The rest of your talk should be focused on this.

Unfortunately, many people focus their talk on themselves. They'll start by telling you that they were founded in 1977, they have X people working for them, out of Y offices in Z countries. It's all a bit me, me, me.

The best way to make sure that you're not doing this is to consider how much you're talking about yourself and how much you're talking about your potential client in your talk. Make it about the benefits to them, rather than your features.

2. Make your talk easy to take in: make it interesting and easy to follow

Whatever you say in a talk, it's your material. If you want your audience to use what you tell them in a way that productively promotes your business, then they have to be able to take it in, remember it and, hopefully, recall it at a later date.

This means that you must make it easy for the audience to understand – and here are three ideas to help you do that.

➤ The first one, **storytelling**, we've already discussed in Chapter 5. Read the chapter if you haven't done so already, but here's a summary:

Stories make it more likely people will listen (because they get emotionally invested in the story), more likely people will remember what you say (for the same reason), and more likely they will recall your story to someone else (because it's human nature to share stories).

Moral: tell stories!

➤ Often when you see a professional speaker talk, they'll **structure** their talk around an easily remembered acronym or model. This makes it easier for the audience to remember the outline of your content – they may not retain every detail, but they will take in the key points because it's easy to remember the structure/model.

When you're putting a talk together, think about hanging your content round a structure. It might be 'The ABC of Sales', 'The VIP Approach to Customer Service' or 'The 5 Step Guide to Getting Your Finances Under Control'.

➤ Your audience won't have heard your talk before, so it's helpful to **signpost** where you are up to. You don't want them to get lost, or not keep up.

Signposting is very simple to do. Assuming you've structured your talk around an ABC model, it simply involves including some linking sentences like this:

'So, we've discussed A and the ramifications for your business. Now let's move on to B, where we'll focus on how to communicate this to your team.'

It's really just saying 'We're done with that section, we're now moving on to the next bit' – but it's amazing how many speakers neglect to do it. If supported by a change in visuals in the PowerPoint, your audience are far more likely to stick with you as you continue your presentation.

3. Make your talk actionable: tell your audience what you want them to do

How many times have you seen a client pitch presentation end with a slide that says: 'Any questions?' What a waste!

Finishing with 'Any questions?' will lead to one of two challenges:

1. The audience ask questions that you either don't want to answer, aren't relevant to anyone else in the audience, or you aren't prepared for. You lose control, which isn't great if you're trying to ensure your presentation is memorable.

   This isn't to say that you shouldn't have a question and answer section in your presentation. My advice is to include it near the end, rather than at the end. That way, you can always bring the talk back to your message, or better still on to the call to action:

2. There's no call to action. If we want to use our speaking to promote our business, then there must be something that they have to do.

    ➤ Do you want them to sign up to something? If so, let them know how.

    ➤ Do you want them to tell their friends/ clients about you? If so, give them a specific instruction.

    ➤ Do you want them to introduce you to someone? If so, who, and how should they do it?

4. Fill your time... but no more

Any time you are asked to speak, you'll be given a certain amount of time. This may be from one minute to one hour – or anywhere in between.

That time is your opportunity, so use it! Not using the entirety of the time to promote your business would be a bit like taking out a newspaper advert and leaving half of it blank.

So, make sure you have the content to fill your time – but don't overrun. It is disrespectful to the organiser of the event, the person that is due to speak after you and the audience if you take more time than you've been allocated.

In fact, you're better off finishing early than late: from the audience's point of view, you're either cutting into the time to hear another speaker (bad), the rest of their day (really bad) or lunch (worst of all).

Think about this when planning and writing your talk. A good rule of thumb is to cut 25 per cent of the content. When you practise and time your talk on your own, you always speak faster and more fluently in your head. When it comes to delivering it to an audience, you will need to speak slower and there's potential for distractions to take up time.

There's good news here though – shortening your talk tends to make it better. TED talks are very deliberately timed at up to 18 minutes, because it forces the speaker to only deliver the very best content (it also puts the talk in the sweet spot for keeping the audience's attention).

Taking the next step with speaking

At the start of this chapter, we discussed the human race's fear of public speaking. Being honest, there's only one way round this – you've just got to give it a go.

I appreciate that this is not as easy as it sounds. My ten-year-old son recently had to go through this exact experience. He had to deliver some lines in his school assembly and was as nervous as anything.

Initially he didn't want to practise and was just asking if we'd let him not go to school on the day in question.

Being ten, there were a lot of tantrums – and to be honest I found it very hard as a parent to comfort him that it would be all right. I was trying to tell him about being out of your comfort zone, about adrenalin, and how afterwards he'd look back and think that it wasn't as hard as he thought it would be. He was having none of it!

He did, reluctantly, start to practise though. As much as anything, I think it was just the fear that as he wasn't going to be allowed to miss school, he couldn't just have nothing to say in front of everyone.

And on the day, when I saw him afterwards, I enthusiastically asked how it went. He nonchalantly announced it had been 'fine', barely looking up from the game he was playing on the iPad.

While he wasn't going to admit as much, there's no question that it wasn't as bad as he thought it was going to be – and it had actually been a good experience to go through.

I think the same will apply to you. As an Unnatural Promoter, I understand how you might be feeling if you've never spoken in public. But you've just got to give it a go. When you commit to something, you've then got the fear that you can't just be up there with nothing to say. So you practise. Then you practise some more.

When you actually deliver your talk – sure, it won't be as perfect as you want it to be – but it won't matter because you've done it. You'll look back, be self-critical, and think of things you'd like to improve. Then you'll move on to the next one – the nerves will kick in again – but you'll get through that too.

Suddenly, without realising it, you'll be speaking in public. I've seen it with thousands of business owners. There's no reason at all why it couldn't happen to you.

Chapter 10: Action Steps

➤ Have a think about how speaking in public will help you to promote your business. What would be advantageous to speak about? Where would be best in terms of providing the right audience?

➤ Write your speech to fill your time, cut 25 per cent of it, then practise, practise, practise.

➤ Go for it!

11 Self-Promotion as an Employee

Throughout this book, we've focused on how to self-promote as an entrepreneur. There has been good news and bad news for Unnatural Promoters in this context: the bad news is you've got to get on and promote yourself – otherwise no one would.

The good news, however, is the big upside if self-promotion is done well. Get your network to shout about you by building great relationships and showing them how they can help you – and you will get opportunities that will help your business develop and grow.

The key point is that you are in control – that is the benefit of being an entrepreneur.

But what of Unnatural Promoters who are employed by someone else? Of course, my instinct as a champion of small business is to encourage everyone into the entrepreneurial world – but being realistic, I recognise that most of the working population are always going to be in the employed sector.

Promotion, of course, means something slightly different within the employment sector. Virtually every organisation has a hierarchical structure of some sort – with different employee and management levels. Job specifications change as you move up, along with, of course, the pay packet and the status within the organisation.

The challenge is that you are not in control: someone else is always going to be making the decision about whether you get promoted or not.

That change in dynamic makes it so uncomfortable for us Unnatural Promoters. Because it is someone else that is making the decision, anything that we do feels like it could be aimed at just influencing the boss.

This would be fine if it was only the boss that saw what we were doing. But the real world is not like that. Usually any decision about promotion will in effect be a competition. If one person moves up, someone else does not.

If one employee is trying to get themselves promoted, then it can come across transparently to their co-workers. Because that means that they could fall behind in the competitive order, sniping and politics both rear their heads.

While Unnatural Promoters don't feel comfortable self-promoting, any Natural Promoters don't have this worry. So they get on with it, and likely as not impress the boss. This then feels doubly unfair! How many times have you seen someone get promoted beyond their capability? It is much worse when you *have* got the ability!

The reality is, though, that if we dwell on other people getting promoted above ourselves, and worrying about politics and what other people think, Unnatural Promoters are never going to get ahead.

We have got to look at this differently – and here I turn back to the entrepreneurial world for inspiration. Throughout this book we have looked at how careful self-promotion, using your network and building good relationships lead to opportunities to meet useful people that can help you grow your business.

As an employee looking to get promoted, the process is exactly the same. If you can carefully self-promote, by using your network and building good relationships, it will lead to opportunities for you to move up in the firm.

Only the outcome is different. For the business owner, the outcome is new business. For the employee, the outcome is promotion. That means the steps that we have discussed in this book are just as relevant to an employee as they are to a business owner.

How to show you're worthy of a promotion

In the same way as an entrepreneur just expecting the phone to ring with business, the employee that thinks they deserve a promotion because they work hard and keep their head down will drastically reduce their chances of getting what they want.

You are much more likely to be successful if you can be more proactive. If you think your boss should be promoting you or giving you a raise, then it is crucial you demonstrate that you are worthy of getting it. Here are 11 ways you can do this.

1. Are you good at your job?

This one probably seems obvious – there's no way you are going to get promoted if you are a poor performer.

If you can, become the team member that everyone goes to for something specific because you're *so* good at it: this will get you noticed by the leaders in the organisation as someone who stands out.

But there are more layers to this than just being good. Remember, if you get promoted, you'll be doing a *different* job, so you have got to demonstrate not only that you are good at what you do now, but are likely to be good at the next level up. That means it is particularly important that you are good at enhancing your knowledge.

2. Are you focused on learning and development?

Again, not difficult to see why this is important, but it's worth exploring a little bit. Your new job will be a different job that will require new responsibilities. If you only ever demonstrate you are very good at your current role, that may persuade your boss that a) you don't have the ability to learn elsewhere or b) that they will lose a valuable asset. One of the most common promotion mistakes is to make the top salesperson the team leader – but that takes away their results while at the same time putting them in a different role that potentially doesn't suit them.

As such, don't be afraid to try out different experiences, even if in the short term it means a sideways move. Volunteer to take on different challenges or learn new ways to deliver in your current role, and that will go a long way to demonstrating that you are not just good at your job, but you also have potential to be even more useful to the organisation.

3. Are you focused on building relationships – with everyone?

We already know that if you want someone to promote you, having a good relationship is a necessary starting point, and it's no different here. Being on good terms with your boss is crucial.

But it isn't just your boss that you need to get on well with. It often won't be *just* your boss making the promotion decision – if you get on well with one person but not the other stakeholders, then there's only so far that your direct boss will go to back you.

This means doing the right thing with everyone – get on with people, treat people with respect, don't gossip about people behind their backs, be a good citizen. That includes co-workers, people in different departments, executive assistants in support roles, janitors, even contractors that come into the office.

At the same time, there are some people in the organisation who will be more important than others when getting promoted. Take networking opportunities when they come up – for example, if there's a group going for a drink after work, or out for lunch. You'll soon be able to see who the influencers are within the company, and who might be able to support you as your career progresses.

4. Are you a good listener?

One of the best ways to build relationships with people across the organisation is to actively listen (or what my other half, Hannah, calls just listening...) This means really tuning in to what people are saying, rather than spending the time considering your response.

Not only will this mean better relationships but it is necessary to do good work too. If you're not listening when your boss is giving instructions – that's not going to end well, is it?

5. Do you set and communicate career goals?

It is worth sitting down with your boss to set and discuss your career goals. Knowing what you want to achieve will make it much more likely to happen because your boss will see you as a motivated individual – attitude is a massive differentiator when considering candidates for an opportunity.

That said, it might seem strange that you would tell your boss that you want to be promoted and how you'd like it to happen. Would they not think that you wanted to take their job?

But if you've built a good relationship with your boss, the chances are they are going to want the best for you as a fellow human being – that might mean they help you by looking out for opportunities in other departments, or giving you the right references to a prospective new boss. Getting promoted won't always be to the pay grade above.

6. Are you a 'yes' person?

Bosses are looking for reliable, dependable people. They want people that will prioritise the team above themselves at times, people who volunteer their efforts before even being asked.

There will often be opportunities to take a new project on, or to help someone else or another team in the office.

Being engaged isn't just about being switched on in meetings. Take these opportunities as they come along.

Sometimes it's not about doing extra work – it might be about saying yes to going on the office social, or to take a new starter out for a coffee to get to know them. Be someone your boss can rely on.

And, of course, once you have said yes, make sure you follow through on the commitment. Not doing so will damage your carefully won reputation.

7. Do you challenge your boss?

That said, just being a 'yes person' isn't what most bosses want. They just want to do the best job they can (either for their superior or the good of the company), so if they have missed something, they'd rather know about it.

There's a huge upside here: you show leadership potential. If you are the person who challenges the project, then you'll stand out among your peers.

So do challenge them. Give them your reasoned argument or stats that make your point. But don't leave them with a problem. Give them a potential fix. This gives another opportunity to demonstrate your ability to think on your own.

8. Are you aware of the bigger picture across the organisation?

When you get promoted, you will naturally have a bigger influence within the whole organisation. To get that opportunity, it is important then that you understand how your current role fits in with other roles and departments.

This allows you to appreciate the culture across the organisation and make more strategic suggestions that will make it more likely you can impress your boss.

9. Do you only ever need to be told something once?

Bosses don't tend to like to have to give out instructions multiple times. Where necessary, note down the tasks so you don't have to commit them to memory. Having that moment as you write things down is also very helpful as you'll have processing time to work out if you need some clarification.

I'm reminded of a boss I once had – he had an autocratic style and used to fire out orders thick and fast. I was listening, but unless I wrote them down I could never recall them all!

10. Do you say the right things, and do you say them well?

What you say and how you say things will make a big difference to how you're perceived in the organisation.

While it can be fun to get involved in office gossip, avoid it at all costs. You never know who is listening or playing political games and reporting back what is being said. If you gossip about someone with your boss (even if they're partaking in the conversation), you've now told them that you're prepared to speak about someone behind their back.

And even in normal office conversation, are you clear and concise with your language, or do you use a lot of 'kinda', 'sorta', 'maybes'? Or are you an 'er', 'um' kind of person? Your boss will be looking for leadership potential and demonstrating your credibility by avoiding these sorts of words will help. Be more concise when talking to your boss than you would be with your peers.

11. Do you make yourself indispensable?

It might seem strange to suggest you should make yourself indispensable. If you are the only person that can do your job, wouldn't that prevent you from moving up as the expense or time taken to find someone else to do your job would be prohibitive?

But this should be taken in a wider context, not just for your position. In his book *The 21 Irrefutable Laws of Leadership*, John C. Maxwell (2007) talks about the Law of Empowerment. He suggests that if you can empower other people to grow and develop, while you will be more dispensable in your own role in the short term, you will quickly become indispensable to the organisation – because of your ability in empowering others.

So you're probably thinking – how on earth can I do all of that? And you're right, there is a lot to think about in that list. But there's a phrase that I think is very pertinent here:

*The way you do anything is
the way you do everything.*

I love this phrase. Looking up the source online, it isn't clear exactly who said it in the first place, but what it's trying to say is that if you don't act in the correct way at all times, it will be apparent. If you show that you'd handle one situation in a given way, that will reflect to the person who sees it that you live your life in that way.

The Unnatural Promoter

That can work positively and negatively. That's why it is so important when it comes to seeking a promotion. Like it or not, you are constantly being judged. It clearly does take time to demonstrate that you have the credibility to move up and lead within the organisation – but you can tear that work down in a moment with the wrong move.

Whoever makes promotion decisions will be looking at whether you show leadership potential. All of the things in the above list are things that good leaders do. Remember – you can't define yourself as a leader: only other people can do this, either because they are happy to follow you as their leader, or because they see you leading others.

Some people choose to make themselves irreplaceable in their role. They make it so no one else can do their job. While this may provide job security, it also pigeonholes them in that role.

Good leaders think about replacing themselves in their current role, so that they can take on the new role. They effectively make themselves redundant. But because it's done in a way that creates another leader, it demonstrates to the ultimate leaders that this is someone who will improve the organisation overall.

This way, you haven't got to play politics or do something just to influence the boss. Instead, everyone is happy. You've been promoted, your colleague who took your job is happy, and your boss is delighted that they've got such a good leader in their ranks who'll help the organisation move forward.

How to ask for a promotion

There are many people who believe that if they keep their heads down, do a good job and work hard, then a promotion will happen. But life isn't like that – you're leaving it to chance.

Clearly, if you're not demonstrating a good number of the traits above, then there is no point even asking. But some proactivity is required. If you would like to be promoted or put yourself in line to be promoted in the future – you've got to ask. Here are a few ways you can make it more likely to happen.

1. Don't ask for a promotion – ask what you have to do to earn a promotion

If your boss doesn't think you're ready to be promoted, when you ask them straight; there's only one answer they can give. It could put them in a difficult position, especially if it feels like a 'promote me or I'll quit' demand.

Instead of asking for a promotion, ask what it would take to be promoted. The answer might be something like 'When you have grown your team by five more people', or 'When your team's sales generate 10 per cent of the company's turnover'.

What have you got then? Something to shoot for, so you can show your boss that you can earn it.

2. Have a business case for your promotion

This ties in closely to showing your boss you've earned your promotion. Once you've done what you set out to do, give facts and data that support what you've achieved. Show your improvement over time, or the difference that you have made to the company.

Listen to the feedback you're given about your progress and demonstrate that you've understood and implemented the advice.

Then, like in sales, you've got to seal the deal, so ask. If the promotion decision can't be made right then and there, or involves other people, then ask when you could expect a decision.

3. Know the right time to ask

It pays to have an appreciation of the wider circumstances the organisation finds itself in. If the economy is making times hard, or there have just been a round of layoffs – it's probably best not to ask then.

A keen appreciation of what is going on in the marketplace will only strengthen your business case when you come to make it.

4. Make your case based on what you have done, not someone else

It is a dangerous game to compare yourself with other people in the organisation. If you think that you should be promoted because one of your colleagues who did get a promotion doesn't do as good a job as you, don't use that as justification.

Worst case, you'll be perceived as unprofessional for criticising the person that promoted them – not just the person that was promoted. That would be particularly bad if it's your boss who will make a decision on you!

Always make your case based on what *you* have achieved.

5. Act in a professional way if it is a 'no for now'

Every year when the Oscars come round, you see the actors that didn't win awards on screen as the winner is announced. They have to come up with a facial expression that says 'well done' to the winner without betraying their disappointment. Not always easy.

It isn't always easy to react in the right way if your boss turns down your request. The best way to look at it is that it is not a 'no' but a 'no for now'. That means you can ask again what it would take to get promoted and make your case at the right time.

The worst thing you can do is to get emotional or throw your toys out of the pram and threaten to quit. Promotion decisions will never just be about the strength of your relationship with your boss – other people will likely be involved – but damaging your relationship with them will paint you as unprofessional and ruin your chances of ever getting the promotion.

Throughout this book we've seen there is much that the entrepreneurial Unnatural Promoter can do to give themselves the best chance of success in their business. It is equally clear that the employed Unnatural Promoter also has the same opportunity.

By demonstrating certain qualities, your boss will be in no doubt that you are ready to be promoted – and then, when the opportunity comes along, there are ways to ask for the promotion that maximise the likelihood of success.

The key point is if people think that they can just keep their head down, work hard and fly under the radar, they will drastically reduce their chances of getting a promotion. Life isn't like that, and as uncomfortable a realisation that is for the Unnatural Promoter, it takes proactivity to get promoted.

Chapter 11: Action Steps

- ➤ Remove the attitude that you just need to work hard to be promoted – realise that you are going to have to be proactive.

- ➤ Set your career goals, and then sit down with your boss to discuss them. Listen to their feedback and adjust as necessary.

- ➤ Volunteer for new experiences, say yes whenever you can, and commit to learning new skills that will make you a better employee.

- ➤ Ask what it will take to earn you a promotion.

- ➤ Once you feel you're ready, build a business case that demonstrates your suitability to be promoted.

Case Study 4
Cornelia Raubal

It was in the middle of a conversation about recruiting a new chief financial officer with her boss that Cornelia Raubal just blurted out:

'I could do that.'

It had almost been without thinking – but then the panic set in, as he replied:

'Great, done.'

She'd got the job, a huge promotion from what she'd been doing before. But how had that even happened? Not only that, but she had been the one that initiated it!

I had always thought of Cornelia Raubal as an entrepreneur. Given that I know her through BNI, where she promotes her executive coaching business, I didn't think about her as an employee.

But when we had a one-to-one over a coffee one day, I found out about her career in the steel industry. If nothing else, our one-to-one was a great advert for getting to know people better. Here I was, thinking of Cornelia as a small business owner, and I found out how she had been a C-level executive in a business turning over hundreds of millions per year!

Being, as she is, a very Unnatural Promoter, Cornelia provides us with a great case study of how to get promoted as an employee.

But first, why is Cornelia such an Unnatural Promoter? When I initially asked her, the quick response came that 'I've always found it difficult'. She told me she hadn't been comfortable as a child and that she had suffered some bullying at school, which means she's always found it hard to share information about herself.

But a big part of her challenge was the fact that most of her career was spent as a woman in the male-dominated steel industry. This led her to feel she had to wear a mask to protect herself from the expectation of what you *should* be like.

Cornelia recalled an incident from very early in her career. She was gaining experience within the industry, running a small team of four working on contracts. One day, a trader within the firm bawled her out in front of everyone in the office for what he perceived to be a mistake.

She had no option but to sit and take it.

Seeking sanctuary in the ladies, Cornelia burst into tears – and various other female employees came in and tried to tell her to just ignore him as he tended to behave like that with people all the time.

That evening, Cornelia went home and talked to her husband about it. Once the initial feelings of hurt had come out, she was surprised that his very direct advice was that she needed to grow up. Fortunately, this isn't a case study in relationship advice!

But she realised her husband was right. Sure, it hadn't been a nice experience – but if she wanted to get ahead in the industry, she *did* need to grow up. What was the alternative? The only other choice was to leave her job and do something completely different.

This was just one example of how Cornelia felt like she had to wear a mask to protect herself in the industry.

So, how did Cornelia manage to be so successful in that industry as an Unnatural Promoter? While it would be lovely if every promotion decision was as easy as the exchange at the start of this case study makes out, that just isn't how it works. Or is it?

When we hear a little bit more about how the promotion to chief financial officer came about, we can see that there were a number of steps that made it happen.

Cornelia had been working in the industry for some time, and while she had had to maintain the mask to protect herself, she'd been successful.

The story started shortly after Cornelia had been made redundant. Attending an industry dinner, Cornelia struck up a conversation with one of the shareholders who was a supplier to the company she'd just been made redundant from.

On hearing about her redundancy, she was immediately offered a role – albeit at a more junior level. Instead of trading and making deals, she was now handling contracts.

However, while trading wasn't in her job specification, Cornelia likes to make things happen for her. So she started to do some trading work alongside the contractual side of her job.

One day, she was asked to do a presentation to all the shareholders of the business at a kick-off meeting. She didn't know it at the time, but no one had ever given the quality of annual report she gave. Her star was rising.

And then, one day, she was in the office with her boss discussing the need to remove the chief financial officer. He wanted ideas of who could be hired as a replacement. It just came out – 'I could do that'.

But while the decision on being promoted was the work of but a few seconds, there were several things that Cornelia had done over time to impress her boss. None of them were done with the intention of being promoted – but they all combined to create the result.

The original offer of a job with the company happened because of Cornelia's networking skills. She had built a relationship as a supplier with her prior company, and then carried that on by engaging in the conversation at the industry dinner. Not only that, the relationship-building continued throughout her time with the firm.

Then, once in the new company, Cornelia did her job well, and proactively looked for ways to do more. Despite only being paid to do contractual work, she helped with trading work, and delivered results. Her presentation to the board only added to her growing status.

Knowing that she is an Unnatural Promoter, we know she wasn't doing all this to impress, she was just doing her job – but her bosses did notice.

Last, but certainly not least – Cornelia had the guts to ask for the promotion when the conversation came up. If she hadn't put herself forward, there's no doubt that someone else would have got the role. You have to be prepared to ask: no one is going to do it for you.

And what about now? Cornelia is no longer in the steel industry and must apply her mask less often these days – but she's still an Unnatural Promoter. When she set up her executive coaching business and put together her website, she was so uncomfortable about self-promoting that she didn't even put a picture of herself on the site, preferring a generic beautiful scenescape instead.

Fortunately, she's come round now – check out **https:// www.craftport.com**.

Once an Unnatural Promoter, Always an Unnatural Promoter

Now that you've reached the end of this book, how are you feeling? Ready to go out there and promote yourself and your business to anyone and everyone?

Thought not. You might now have got a range of strategies and tools to help you – but that doesn't necessarily make it easier. For my part, I'm never going to be anything other than an Unnatural Promoter – it will always feel a bit uncomfortable.

However, remind yourself of the key point in this book: if you don't enjoy talking about yourself, or you don't have the confidence to stick your head above the parapet the whole time, get other people to do it for you! Networking is great – instead of having to talk about you and your business to everyone, just pick a few key people, build relationships with them, and they'll go out and shout about you to people they know.

Doing business by relationship isn't just a strategy to help Unnatural Promoters. It's a great way of living your life!

But I'd like to finish with a reference from Derren Brown, the mentalist and illusionist; you may have seen him blowing your mind on television. In his book *Happy* (2017), he outlines the secret magical formula to success. It's very simple: talent + energy. That's it. You can have all the talent in the world, but if you don't get it out there, it will do you no good at all.

I know that you, as an Unnatural Promoter, have got the talent. You just need to be brave and tell some people about it.

What's your networking strategy going to be?

Having read this book, it should be clear that BNI has been an important part of my life. But I would go further to suggest that BNI is a great place for any Unnatural Promoter.

Think about it – I'm encouraging you to:

➤ build relationships with a manageable group of people

➤ understand why you do what you do

➤ tell your business story regularly

➤ be ultra-specific in what you are targeting in your business

➤ prioritise building relationships on a one-to-one basis

➤ be strategic with networking and work with related businesses to yours that can help you the most

➤ connect with others via the power of social media

> ➤ deliver your message effectively by speaking well in public.

BNI is great at delivering all of these, and it is wrapped up with a set of values that means you get a supporting team holding you accountable to do what it takes to make the promotion of your business work for you.

See you there!

Bibliography

99firms (2021). 'LinkedIn Statistics'. Available at: **www.99firms.com/blog/linkedin-statistics/**

Ahlgren, M. (2021). '40+ Instagram statistics and facts for 2020'. Website Hosting Rating. Available at: **www.websitehosting rating.com/instagram-statistics/**

Ayres, M. (2017). 'The science behind why no one likes to be on camera'. Wistia. Available at: **www.wistia.com/learn/production/science-behind-being-on-camera**

Axtell, P. (2019). 'The most productive meetings have fewer than 8 people'. *Harvard Business Review*. Available at: **www.hbr.org/2018/06/the-most-productive-meetings-have-fewer-than-8-people**

Barnard, D. (2018). 'Average speaking rate and words per minute'. VirtualSpeech. Available at: **www.virtualspeech.com/blog/average-speaking-rate-words-per-minute**

Bounds, A. (2010). *The Jelly Effect*. Capstone.

Brown, D. (2017). *Happy*. Corgi.

Cialdini, R. (2007). *Influence: The Psychology of Persuasion*. HarperBus.

Fritscher, L. (2020). 'Glossophobia or the fear of public speaking'. Verywell Mind 6/10/2020. Available at: **www.verywellmind.com/glossophobia-2671860**

Gallant, J. (2021). '50+ LinkedIn statistics marketers need to know in 2021'. Foundation. Available at: **www.foundationinc.co/lab/b2b-marketing-linkedin-stats/**

Hall, J.A. (2018). 'How many hours does it take to make a friend?'. *Journal of Social and Personal Relationships* 36(4). Available at: **journals.sagepub.com/doi/full/10.1177/0265407518761225**

Kermode, R. (2013). *Speak: So Your Audience Will Listen*. Pendle Publishing.

Lawson, C. (2014). *The Unnatural Networker*. Panoma Press.

LinkedIn (2017). The Sophisticated Marketer's Guide to LinkedIn. Available at: **www.business.linkedin.com/content/dam/me/ business/en-us/marketing-solutions/cx/2017/pdfs/Sophisti- cated-Marketers-Guide-to-Linked In-v03.12.pdf**

Maxwell, J.C. (2007). *The 21 Irrefutable Laws of Leadership*. Thomas Nelson.

Misner, I., Walker, H. & DeRaffele, F. (2012). *Business Networking and Sex (Not What You Think)*. Entrepreneur Press.

Sinek, S. (2011). *Start with Why*. Penguin.

Sinek, S., Mead, D. et al. (2017). *Find your Why*. Portfolio Penguin.

Statista (2016). 'Share of brands that have an Instagram profile as of March 2016, by category'. Available at: **www.statista.com/statistics/305292/worldwide- instagram-brand-adoption-rate-category**

Statista (2021). 'Distribution of Instagram users worldwide as of January 2021, by age and gender'. Available at: **www.statista.com/statistics/248769/age-distribution- of-worldwide-instagram-users**

Thomas, B. (2020). *Watertight Marketing*. Human Business Thinking.

Townsend, H. (2014). *The Financial Times Guide to Business Networking*. FT Publishing International.

Wohlsen, M. (2014). 'The next big thing you missed: LinkedIn's quest to get a job for everyone on earth'. *Wired* 11/11/2014. Available at **www.wired.com/2014/11/next-big-thing-missed-linkedins- quest-get-job-everyone-earth/**

BNI

BNI is the most successful business networking referral organisation in the world. There are over 275,000 members across over 10,000 chapters globally, and in the UK and Ireland alone, in 2020 business was passed to the value of close to half a billion pounds, despite the world being in the grip of the Covid-19 pandemic. It is quite literally the best way to build a better business.

BNI's philosophy is Givers Gain, which is simply this: 'If I give you business, you'll want to give me business.'

BNI allows only one representative from each trade or profession to join any BNI group. This means you can lock out your competition, ensuring you receive 100 per cent of all new business.

BNI teaches its members how to attract and win more new business for each other through word of mouth. Working together, BNI members achieve incredible results, growing their business in ways they could never accomplish alone.

To find your nearest BNI meeting, go to **www.bni.co.uk**.